Block Buster QUILTS

I Love Star Blocks

16 Quilts from an All-Time Favorite Block

Compiled by Karen M. Burns

Martingale
Create with Confidence

Block-Buster Quilts
I Love Star Blocks: 16 Quilts from an All-Time Favorite Block
© 2017 by Martingale & Company®

Martingale®
19021 120th Ave. NE, Ste. 102
Bothell, WA 98011-9511 USA
ShopMartingale.com

Printed in China
22 21 20 19 18 17   8 7 6 5 4 3 2 1

Library of Congress Cataloging-in-Publication Data is available upon request.

ISBN: 978-1-60468-856-6

MISSION STATEMENT

We empower makers who use fabric and yarn to make life more enjoyable.

CREDITS

**PUBLISHER AND
CHIEF VISIONARY OFFICER**
Jennifer Erbe Keltner

CONTENT DIRECTOR
Karen Costello Soltys

MANAGING EDITOR
Tina Cook

ACQUISITIONS EDITOR
Karen M. Burns

TECHNICAL EDITORS
Beth Bradley
Deb Finan

COPY EDITOR
Melissa Bryan

DESIGN MANAGER
Adrienne Smitke

**COVER AND
INTERIOR DESIGNER**
Regina Girard

PHOTOGRAPHER
Brent Kane

ILLUSTRATOR
Sandy Huffaker

Contents

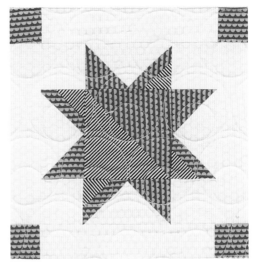

Introduction

You have stars in your eyes. I'm seeing stars. Here's the star attraction. Oh my stars! Now starring...

You don't have to think long to come up with phrases that include stars in them, sayings that are all a part of our everyday life. Nor do you have to look far when combing through favorite quilts and patterns to find those that include Star blocks.

Perennial favorites of quilters for centuries, Star blocks shine as brightly today as they ever did. And this collection of quilt patterns showcases them in myriad ways. What I enjoy most is the diversity of star styles and how you can match them with the personality of your quilt recipient. Looking for a quilt pattern to fete a superstar in your midst? Check out Big Star on page 64. Or would you prefer to recognize a hidden star who stays behind the scenes? If so, Hazelwood Stars on page 50 might just fit the bill. How about making County Fair on page 27 for a special friend or family member—the kind who radiates star power in all they do? Know someone who sparkles all the time from dawn to dusk? Maybe Sunrise, Sunset on page 9 is the quilt for that bright personality. Or would you like to honor a veteran for his or her service? Cozy Stars on page 14, with its regimented rows of stars, might be just the pattern you need.

One thing I'm certain of is this: You're sure to have the right Star block for every quilt occasion with this book in hand. So whether the stars are out tonight or not, curl up with this good book and start dreaming of your next quilt. And if it ends up being one you make for your own bed? Well, then you'll be sleeping under the stars for the foreseeable future.

Star power is packed in these pages!

Jennifer Keltner,
Publisher and Chief Visionary Officer

Star Block Basics

Star blocks have been around as long as quiltmaking itself, so there just might be enough different Star blocks to populate a whole galaxy.

One of the most iconic star motifs in quilting is the basic eight-pointed star. Even within the eight-pointed star category, dozens of variations exist. As with many other common blocks, you can take your pick of various methods for constructing an eight-pointed star depending on the look you want to achieve. Here, we'll focus on two classic eight-pointed star blocks: the Sawtooth Star and the LeMoyne Star.

Sawtooth Star

The Sawtooth Star is a fun and simple block that requires flying-geese units for the points. The following assembly method comes in handy because it yields four flying-geese units at once. To calculate the size of the pieces to cut, use this formula:

★ Size to cut large square = desired finished length of flying geese + 1¼". For a finished 3" × 6" unit, the large square should be 7¼".

★ Size to cut small squares = desired finished height of flying geese + ⅞". For a finished 3" × 6" unit, the small squares should be 3⅞".

1. Cut one large light square and four small dark squares according to the formulas above. In addition to the pieces for the flying geese, cut one square for the star center and four squares for the corners. The center square is the same size as the length of the flying-geese units. In this case, 6" finished. So cut a 6½" square. The corner squares are the same size as the height

of the flying-geese units. In this example, 3" finished. So cut four 3½" squares.

2. Draw a diagonal line from corner to corner on the wrong side of the four small squares. Place marked squares on opposite corners of the large square with right sides together as shown. The corners of the small squares will overlap slightly and the drawn lines should extend across the large square from corner to corner. Sew ¼" from both sides of the line.

3. Cut along the drawn line, and then press the seam allowances toward the small triangles.

4. Place a marked square on the corner of each unit from step 3 with right sides together,

orienting the line as shown, from the corner to the point between the two triangles. Sew ¼" from both sides of the marked line.

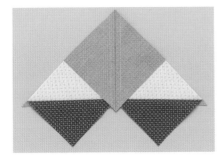

5. Cut along each drawn line, yielding two units each for a total of four units. Press the seam allowances toward the small triangles.

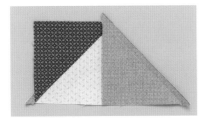

6. Lay out the flying-geese units, small squares, and center square in three rows. Join the units in each row; press the seam allowances toward the squares. Join the rows; press the seam allowances toward the center. The Sawtooth Star block should measure 12½" square, including seam allowances.

LeMoyne Star

The LeMoyne Star is another common eight-pointed star block. Here's an easy assembly method that uses only squares and half-square-triangle units, rather than the traditional diamond-shaped pieces and set-in seams.

1. To make a 12" finished block (12½" with seam allowances), cut four light 3½" squares for the corners and four light 3⅞" squares for the background of the star points. Additionally, cut four medium 3⅞" squares and four dark 3⅞" squares for the star points.

2. Draw a line from corner to corner on the wrong side of the medium squares. Place a medium and a light 3⅞" square right sides together. Sew ¼" from both sides of the marked line. Cut along the line to yield two half-square-triangle units. Press the seam allowances toward the darker fabric. Trim the units to measure 3½" square, including seam allowances. Repeat to make four matching half-square-triangle units.

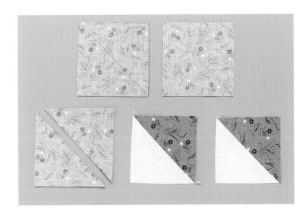

3. Repeat step 2 using light and dark squares to make four light/dark half-square-triangle units and four medium/dark half-square-triangle units. In total, you'll have 12 half-square-triangle units.

4. Lay out the light squares and half-square-triangle units in four rows of four, orienting them as shown to create the star design. Join the units in each row; press the seam allowances in opposite directions from row to row.

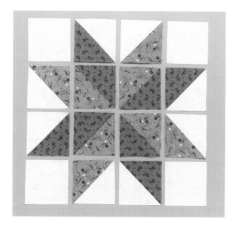

5. Join the rows; press the seam allowances in one direction. The LeMoyne Star block should measure 12½" square, including seam allowances.

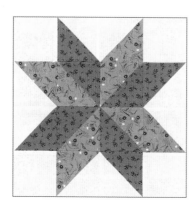

CHANGE IT UP

The Eight-Pointed Star layout is very simple, so it allows for a great deal of variation depending on placement of colors or light and dark values. Check out the following examples of alternative Star options and be inspired to design your own unique blocks.

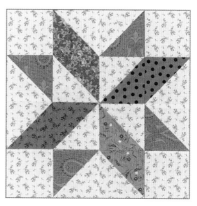

Sunrise, Sunset

Materials

Yardage is based on 42"-wide fabric.

1 yard of dark blue tone on tone for blocks
⅜ yard of medium blue tone on tone for blocks
⅜ yard of light blue tone on tone for blocks
⅝ yard of medium orange tone on tone for blocks
⅝ yard of light orange tone on tone for blocks
1¼ yards of dark orange tone on tone for blocks
1½ yards of gray tone on tone for blocks and binding
4 yards of white tone on tone for background
7¾ yards of fabric for backing
92" × 92" piece of batting

Cutting

All measurements include ¼" seam allowances.

From *each* of the medium blue and light blue tone on tones, cut:
★ 3 strips, 3½" × 42" (6 total)

From the dark blue tone on tone, cut:
★ 8 strips, 3⅞" × 42"; crosscut into 80 squares, 3⅞" × 3⅞"

From *each* of the medium orange and light orange tone on tones, cut:
★ 5 strips, 3½" × 42" (10 total)

From the dark orange tone on tone, cut:
★ 10 strips, 3⅞" × 42"; crosscut into 100 squares, 3⅞" × 3⅞"

From the gray tone on tone, cut:
★ 5 strips, 4¾" × 42"; crosscut into 40 squares, 4¾" × 4¾"
★ 9 strips, 2½" × 42"

From the white tone on tone, cut:
★ 9 strips, 7¼" × 42"; crosscut into 45 squares, 7¼" × 7¼"
★ 8 strips, 3⅞" × 42"; crosscut into 80 squares, 3⅞" × 3⅞".
   Cut the squares in half diagonally to yield 160 triangles.
★ 10 strips, 3½" × 42"; crosscut into 100 squares, 3½" × 3½"

Alternating Four-Patch Star blocks with Diamond blocks creates a dynamic composition. Sunny orange and yellow prints paired with cool shades of blue make a quilt that brings to mind dawn and dusk.

Sunrise, Sunset by Melissa Corry

FINISHED QUILT: 84½" × 84½"
FINISHED BLOCK: 12" × 12"

Making the Four-Patch Units

Press all seam allowances as indicated by the arrows.

1. Join a medium blue strip and a light blue strip along the long edges. Make three strip sets. From each strip set, cut 11 segments, 3½" wide, for a total of 33 segments (1 is extra).

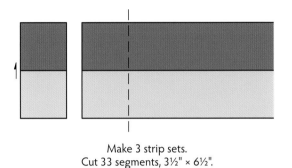

Make 3 strip sets.
Cut 33 segments, 3½" × 6½".

2. Join a medium orange strip and a light orange strip along the long edges. Make five strip sets. From each strip set, cut 10 segments, 3½" wide, for a total of 50 segments.

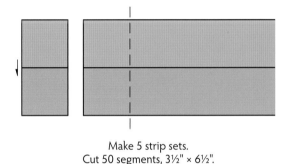

Make 5 strip sets.
Cut 50 segments, 3½" × 6½".

3. Lay out two blue segments, alternating the placement of the medium and light patches as shown. Join the segments. The four-patch unit should measure 6½" square, including seam allowances. Repeat to make 16 blue four-patch units.

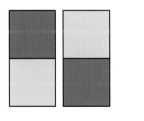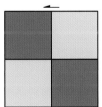

Make 16 units,
6½" × 6½".

4. Repeat the process from step 3 using the orange strip-set segments. Make 25 orange four-patch units measuring 6½" square, including seam allowances.

Make 25 units,
6½" × 6½".

Making the Square-in-a-Square Units

Lay out four white triangles around one gray square as shown. Sew triangles to two opposite sides of the square; press, and then sew triangles to the two remaining sides of the square. Repeat to make 40 units that measure 6½" square, including seam allowances.

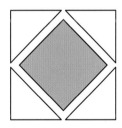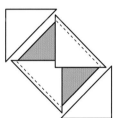

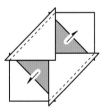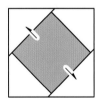

Make 40 units,
6½" × 6½".

Making the Flying-Geese Units

1. Place dark orange 3⅞" squares on opposite corners of a white 7¼" square with right sides together, aligning the edges as shown. Draw a diagonal line from the top-left corner to the bottom-right corner of the dark orange squares. Stitch ¼" from both sides of the drawn line. Cut along the drawn line to yield two units.

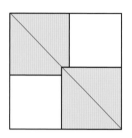 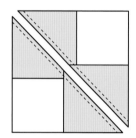

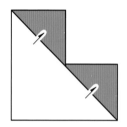

2. Draw a diagonal line from corner to corner on the wrong side of a dark orange 3⅞" square. Place the marked square on the corner of one of the units from step 1 with right sides together, aligning raw edges as shown. Stitch ¼" from both sides of the drawn line. Cut along the line to yield two flying-geese units. The units should measure 3½" × 6½", including seam allowances. Repeat to make 100 flying-geese units.

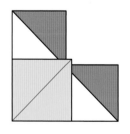 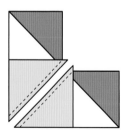

Make 100 units,
3½" × 6½".

3. Repeat steps 1 and 2 using the remaining white 7¼" squares and the dark blue 3⅞" squares to make 80 flying-geese units that measure 3½" × 6½", including seam allowances.

Make 80 units,
3½" × 6½".

Making the Diamond Blocks and Star Blocks

1. Lay out one square-in-a-square unit and two dark blue flying-geese units as shown. Sew the flying-geese units to the top and bottom of the square-in-a-square unit. The block should measure 6½" × 12½", including seam allowances. Repeat to make 40 Diamond blocks.

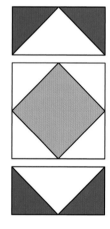 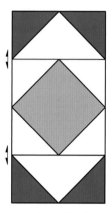

Make 40 blocks,
6½" × 12½".

2. Lay out an orange four-patch unit, four white 3½" squares, and four orange flying-geese units in three rows as shown. Join the units in each row, and then join the rows. The block should measure 12½" square, including seam allowances. Repeat to make 25 Star blocks.

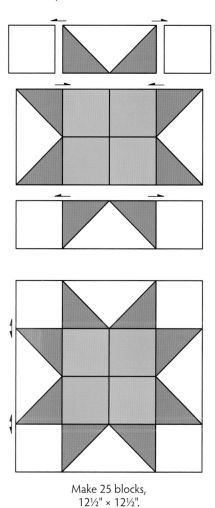

Make 25 blocks,
12½" × 12½".

Assembling the Quilt Top

1. Lay out five Star blocks and four Diamond blocks, alternating them as shown. Join the blocks into a row measuring 12½" × 84½", including seam allowances. Repeat to make five Star rows.

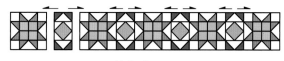

Make 5 rows,
12½" × 84½".

2. Lay out five Diamond blocks horizontally, alternating them with four blue four-patch units as shown. Join the blocks into a row measuring 6½" × 84½", including seam allowances. Repeat to make four Diamond rows.

Make 4 rows,
6½" × 84½".

3. Lay out the Star and Diamond rows, alternating them as shown in the quilt assembly diagram. Join the rows. The finished quilt top should measure 84½" square.

Quilt assembly

Finishing the Quilt

Go to ShopMartingale.com/HowtoQuilt for more details on quilting and finishing.

1. Layer the backing, batting, and quilt top; baste the layers together. Hand or machine quilt. The quilt shown is machine quilted with an allover swirl design.

2. Use the gray 2½"-wide strips to make the binding and then attach it to the quilt.

Pretty Star blocks twinkle within a flying-geese frame in a charming vintage-inspired quilt design. Use dotted fabrics to add a modern touch to the classic color scheme.

Cozy Stars

Materials

Yardage is based on 42"-wide fabric.

3¼ yards of white solid for blocks and borders
2¾ yards of blue dot for blocks, outer border, and binding
1⅞ yards of red-on-cream dot for blocks
3⅞ yards of fabric for backing
69" × 79" piece of batting

Cutting

All measurements include ¼" seam allowances.

From the *lengthwise* grain of the white solid, cut:
★ 2 strips, 3" × 60½"
★ 2 strips, 3" × 55½"

From the remainder of the white solid, cut:
★ 220 squares, 3" × 3"
★ 240 rectangles, 1¾" × 3"

From the blue dot, cut:
★ 9 strips, 5½" × 42"; crosscut into:
    30 squares, 5½" × 5½"
    48 rectangles, 3" × 5½"
★ 11 strips, 1¾" × 42"; crosscut into 240 squares, 1¾" × 1¾"
★ 8 strips, 2½" × 42"

From the red-on-cream dot, cut:
★ 18 strips, 3" × 42"; crosscut into:
    120 rectangles, 3" × 4¼"
    120 rectangles, 1¾" × 3"

Making the Blocks

Press all seam allowances as indicated by the arrows.

1. Draw a diagonal line from corner to corner on the wrong side of the white 3" squares. Place a marked square on the left end of a red 3" × 4¼" rectangle with right sides together, orienting the drawn line as shown. Sew on the drawn line, and then trim ¼" from the seam. Repeat to make 60 left folded-corner units.

Make 60 units,
3" × 4¼".

Cozy Stars by Kimberly Jolly; pieced by Nova Birchfield; quilted by Diane Selman of mylongarm.com

FINISHED QUILT: 60½" × 70½"

FINISHED BLOCK: 10" × 10"

2. Repeat the process from step 1, but place the white square on the opposite end of the red rectangle and orient the line as shown. Make 60 right folded-corner units.

Make 60 units,
3" × 4¼".

3. Draw a diagonal line from corner to corner on the wrong side of the blue 1¾" squares. Place a marked square on a white rectangle with right sides together, orienting the line as shown. Sew on the drawn line, and then trim ¼" from the seam. Repeat to sew a second marked square to the opposite end of the rectangle. Repeat to make 120 flying-geese units that measure 1¾" × 3", including seam allowances.

Make 120 units,
1¾" × 3".

4. Sew a white rectangle to the top (white edge) of a flying-geese unit as shown. Make 120 units that measure 3" square, including seam allowances.

Make 120 units,
3" × 3".

5. Sew red 1¾" × 3" rectangles to opposite sides of a unit from step 4. Make 60 side units that measure 3" × 5½", including seam allowances.

Make 120 units,
3" × 5½".

6. Lay out two left and two right folded-corner units, two pieced squares, two side units, and a blue 5½" square. Join the units into three rows, and then join the rows to complete the Cozy Star block. Make 30 blocks that measure 10½" square, including seam allowances.

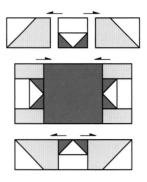 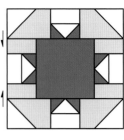

Make 30 blocks,
10½" × 10½".

Assembling the Quilt Top

1. Lay out the blocks in six rows of five as shown. Join the blocks in each row, and then join the rows. The quilt center should measure 50½" × 60½", including seam allowances.

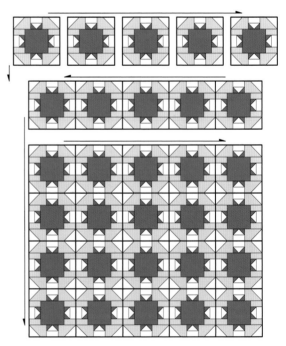

Quilt assembly

2. For the flying-geese outer border, draw a diagonal line from corner to corner on the wrong side of two white 3" squares. Place a marked square right sides together on one end of a blue rectangle, orienting the line as shown. Sew on the marked line. Trim ¼" from the seam and press. In the same manner, sew the second marked square to the opposite end of the rectangle to complete a flying-geese unit. Repeat to make 48 units that measure 3" × 5½", including seam allowances.

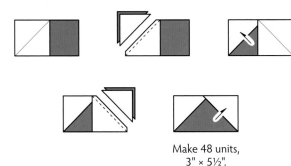

Make 48 units,
3" × 5½".

3. To make the top and bottom border strips, join 11 flying-geese units each along the short edges as shown. Sew white 3" squares to the ends of the border strips, which should measure 3" × 60½", including seam allowances. To make the side border strips, join 13 flying-geese units each. Make two strips that measure 3" × 65½", including seam allowances.

Make 2 top/bottom borders,
3" × 60½".

Make 2 side borders,
3" × 65½".

4. Sew the white 60½"-long strips to the sides of the quilt center, and then sew the white 55½"-long strips to the top and bottom. The quilt top should now measure 55½" × 65½", including seam allowances.

5. Sew the pieced side border strips to the quilt top, and then add the pieced top and bottom border strips. The finished quilt top should measure 60½" × 70½".

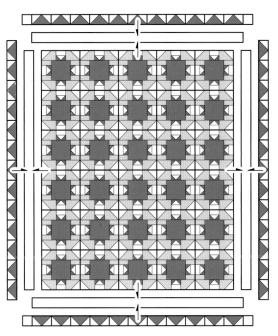

Adding borders

Finishing the Quilt

Go to ShopMartingale.com/HowtoQuilt for more details on quilting and finishing.

1. Layer the backing, batting, and quilt top; baste the layers together. Hand or machine quilt. The quilt shown is machine quilted with an allover swirl and curl design.

2. Use the blue 2½"-wide strips to make the binding and then attach it to the quilt.

Autumn Star

Lynne's layered patchwork technique makes adding the curved pieces to the Star block much easier than it looks. There are no curved seams to sew in the faux sashing, either. Give her technique a try!

Materials

Yardage is based on 42"-wide fabric. Fat quarters measure 18" × 21".

1 yard of tan dot for block background and inner border
1⅛ yards of navy print for star points, outer border, and binding
1 fat quarter of tan floral for block centers
½ yard of red print for melon pieces
2¾ yards of fabric for backing
48" × 48" piece of batting
Fusible web
Fabric glue stick

Cutting

All measurements include ¼" seam allowances.

From the tan dot, cut:
★ 7 strips, 3½" × 42"; crosscut *4 strips* into 36 rectangles, 3½" × 4½", and *3 strips* into 36 squares, 3½" × 3½"
★ 2 strips, 2" × 33½"
★ 2 strips, 2" × 30½"

From the navy print, cut:
★ 8 strips, 2½" × 42"; crosscut *3 strips* into 36 squares, 2½" × 2½". Cut the squares in half diagonally to yield 72 triangles.
★ 2 strips, 4½" × 41½"
★ 2 strips, 4½" × 33½"

From the tan floral, cut:
★ 9 squares, 4½" × 4½"

Autumn Star by Lynne Hagmeier
FINISHED QUILT: 41½" × 41½"
FINISHED BLOCK: 10" × 10"

Making the Blocks

Press all seam allowances as indicated by the arrows.

1. Place two navy triangles right side up on the right side of a tan dot rectangle, positioning the triangles at the bottom of the rectangle as shown. Secure the triangles with a small amount of glue. Topstitch ⅛" from the long raw edge of each triangle using matching navy thread. In this technique, the triangle edges are left raw, but won't ravel because they've been cut on the bias. Repeat to make 36 star-point units that measure 3½" × 4½", including seam allowances.

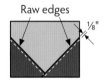

Raw edges
⅛"

Make 36 units,
3½" × 4½".

2. Lay out four star-point units, four tan dot squares, and one tan floral square in three rows of three as shown. Join the units in each row, and then join the rows. The block should measure 10½" square, including seam allowances. Make nine blocks.

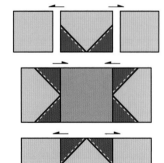

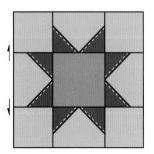

Make 9 blocks,
10½" × 10½".

3. Using the pattern on page 21, trace the melon shape 192 times onto the paper backing of the fusible web. Adhere the fusible web to the wrong side of the red fat quarter. Cut out the melons along the drawn line, and then peel away the paper backing.

4. Place eight melons right side up on one block, centering them over the seams of the center square as shown. Following the manufacturer's instructions, fuse the melons in place. Stitch ⅛" inside the edges of each melon using matching red thread. Repeat to sew melons to each block.

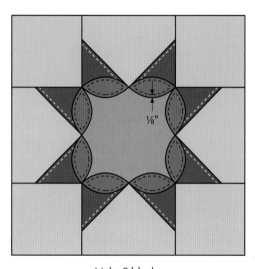

⅛"

Make 9 blocks.

Assembling the Quilt Top

1. Lay out the blocks in three rows of three. Join the blocks in each row, and then join the rows. The quilt center should measure 30½" square, including seam allowances.

2. Sew the tan 30½"-long strips to the sides of the quilt top, and then add the tan 33½"-long strips to the top and bottom. The quilt top should now measure 33½" square, including seam allowances.

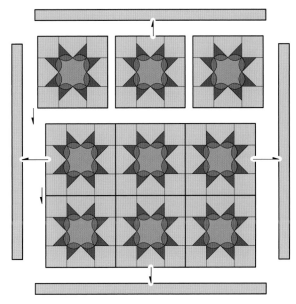

Quilt assembly

3. Center five melons over each 10" block seam, and then fuse them in place. Using matching red thread and a ⅛" seam allowance, sew the edges of all the melons continuously from top to bottom and side to side.

4. Sew the navy 33½"-long strips to the sides of the quilt top, and then add the navy 41½"-long strips to the top and bottom. The finished quilt top should measure 41½" square.

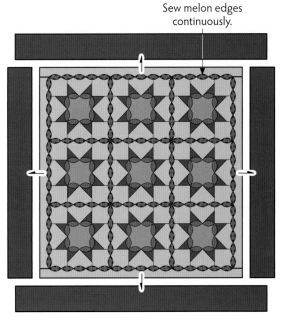

Adding borders

Finishing the Quilt

Go to ShopMartingale.com/HowtoQuilt for more details on quilting and finishing.

1. Layer the backing, batting, and quilt top; baste the layers together. Hand or machine quilt. The quilt shown is machine quilted in the ditch around all of the star points, and then a double circle is stitched around each block. The corners of the blocks are quilted with a feather motif.

2. Use the remaining navy 2½"-wide strips to make the binding and then attach it to the quilt.

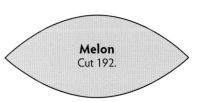

Melon
Cut 192.

Shoofly Star

Sue spiced up a classic Star block by placing a Shoofly block in the center. Add variety to the simple one-block quilt design by choosing a different color combination for each block.

Materials

Yardage is based on 42"-wide fabric. Fat quarters measure 18" × 21".

15 fat quarters of assorted medium and dark prints for blocks (collectively referred to as *dark*)
½ yard *each* of 8 assorted cream prints for block backgrounds
⅔ yard of red plaid for inner border
2⅛ yards of red floral for outer border and binding
7 yards of fabric for backing
84" × 97" piece of batting

Cutting

All measurements include ¼" seam allowances.

From *each* of the 15 dark print fat quarters, cut:
★ 1 strip, 5" × 22"; crosscut into 4 squares, 5" × 5" (60 total)*
★ 4 strips, 3" × 22"; crosscut into 26 squares, 3" × 3" (390 total)*

From *each* of the 8 assorted cream prints, cut:
★ 5 strips, 3" × 42"; crosscut into:
★ 16 strips, 3" × 8" (128 total; 8 are extra)**
★ 16 squares, 3" × 3" (128 total; 8 are extra)**

From the red plaid, cut:
★ 8 strips, 2½" × 42"

From the red floral, cut:
★ 8 strips, 5" × 42"
★ 8 strips, 2½" × 42"

Sort the pieces from each dark print into 2 matching sets of one 5" square and four 3" squares, and 2 matching sets of one 5" square and nine 3" squares.

**Sort the pieces from each cream print into 30 matching sets of four 3" × 8" strips and four 3" squares (2 sets are extra).*

Shoofly Star by Sue Pfau

FINISHED QUILT: 76" × 88½"
FINISHED BLOCK: 12½" × 12½"

Making the Blocks

Press all seam allowances as indicated by the arrows.

1. Select the following pieces for each block, using matching fabrics for each set:
   - ★ Set A (dark): one 5" square, four 3" squares
   - ★ Set B (dark): one 5" square, nine 3" squares
   - ★ Set C (cream): four 3" x 8" strips, four 3" squares

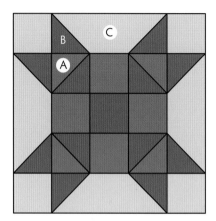

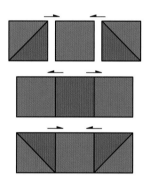

BEWARE OF STRETCHY FABRIC

When making half-square-triangle units in step 2, above right, the outer edges of the units end up cut on the bias. To keep them from stretching out of shape, press the units to set the seam, and then use the tip of the iron to open up the half-square triangles. Press along the seam, gently moving toward the corners with the tip of the iron. When sewing a half-square-triangle unit into the shoofly unit, place the half-square-triangle unit on the bottom against the machine's feed dogs, which will help feed the fabric evenly.

2. Place a 5" A square and a 5" B square right sides together. Sew around the perimeter of the squares, ¼" from the edges. Cut the squares into quarters diagonally to yield four half-square-triangle units. Trim the units to measure 3" square, including seam allowances. Handle these units with care, as the outer edges will all be on the bias.

Make 4 units.

3. Lay out the four half-square-triangle units from step 2, four 3" A squares, and one 3" B square in three rows as shown. Join the units in each row, and then join the rows. The shoofly unit should measure 8" square, including seam allowances.

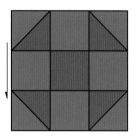

Make 1 unit,
8" × 8".

4. Draw a diagonal line on the wrong side of the remaining eight 3" B squares. Place a marked square on each end of a cream strip with right sides together, orienting the lines as shown. Sew on the lines, and then trim the seam

allowances to ¼". Make four units measuring 3" × 8", including seam allowances.

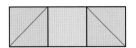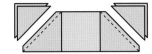

Make 4 units,
3" × 8".

5. Sew one 3" C square to each end of two of the units from step 4. The units should measure 3" × 13", including seam allowances.

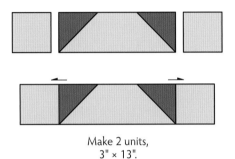

Make 2 units,
3" × 13".

6. Sew the two remaining units from step 4 to opposite sides of the shoofly unit from step 3. The unit should measure 8" × 13", including seam allowances.

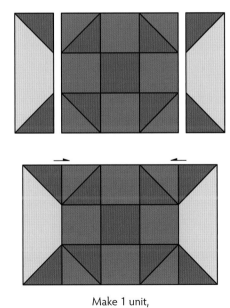

Make 1 unit,
8" × 13".

7. Sew the units from step 5 to the top and bottom of the shoofly unit. The block should measure 13" square, including seam allowances. Repeat to make 30 blocks.

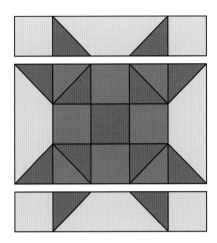

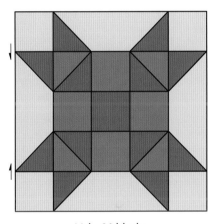

Make 30 blocks,
13" × 13".

Assembling the Quilt Top

1. Lay out the blocks in six rows of five, as shown in the quilt assembly diagram below. Join the blocks in each row, and then join the rows. The quilt center should measure 63" × 75½", including seam allowances.

2. Join the red plaid 2½"-wide strips end to end. From the pieced length, cut two strips, 75½" long, for the side borders and two strips, 67" long, for the top and bottom borders. Sew the side borders to the quilt top first, and then add the top and bottom borders. The quilt top should now measure 67" × 79½", including seam allowances.

3. Join the red floral 5"-wide strips end to end. From the pieced length, cut two strips, 79½" long, for the side borders and two strips, 76" long, for the top and bottom borders. Sew the side borders to the quilt top first, and then add the top and bottom borders. The finished quilt top should measure 76" × 88½".

Finishing the Quilt

Go to ShopMartingale.com/HowtoQuilt for more details on quilting and finishing.

1. Layer the backing, batting, and quilt top; baste the layers together. Hand or machine quilt. The quilt shown is machine quilted with an allover feather and swirl pattern in the quilt center and a feather pattern in the borders.

2. Use the red floral 2½"-wide strips to make the binding and then attach it to the quilt.

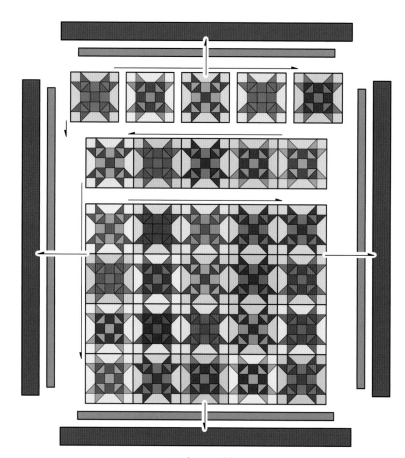

Quilt assembly

County Fair

Materials

Yardage is based on 42"-wide fabric. Fat quarters measure 18" × 21".

20 to 28 fat quarters of assorted bright blue, orange, red, and yellow prints for blocks*
6 yards of white solid for background
⅔ yard of blue floral for binding
7⅜ yards of fabric for backing
88" × 88" piece of batting

Use more fat quarters for greater variety.

Cutting

All measurements include ¼" seam allowances.

From the bright print fat quarters, cut a scrappy assortment of:
★ 36 squares, 7¼" × 7¼"
★ 36 squares, 4" × 4"
★ 36 squares, 3½" × 3½"
★ 16 squares, 2½" × 2½"

From the white solid, cut:
★ 15 strips, 3⅞" × 42"; crosscut into 144 squares, 3⅞" × 3⅞"
★ 17 strips, 3½" × 42"; crosscut into 180 squares, 3½" × 3½"
★ 24 strips, 2½" × 24½"
★ 4 strips, 4" × 42"; crosscut into 36 squares, 4" × 4"

From the blue floral, cut:
★ 9 strips, 2½" × 42"

The cheerful colors and playful design of this scrappy quilt bring to mind a summertime carnival. Two variations of an extra-large Star block create the fun, dynamic composition.

County Fair by Melissa Corry

FINISHED QUILT: 80½" × 80½"
FINISHED BLOCK: 24" × 24"

Making the Half-Square-Triangle Units

Press all seam allowances as indicated by the arrows.

Draw a diagonal line on the wrong side of the white 4" squares. Place a marked square right sides together with a print 4" square. Sew ¼" from both sides of the drawn line. Cut along the drawn line to yield two half-square-triangle units. Using the seamline as a guide, trim the units to measure 3½" square, including seam allowances. Repeat to make 72 units.

Make 72 units.

Making the Flying-Geese Units

1. Place white 3⅞" squares on opposite corners of a print 7¼" square with right sides together, aligning the edges as shown. Draw a diagonal line from the top-left corner to the bottom-right corner. Sew ¼" from both sides of the drawn line. Cut along the drawn line to yield two units.

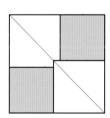

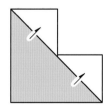

2. Draw a diagonal line from corner to corner on the wrong side of a white 3⅞" square. Place the marked square on the corner of one of the step 1 units with right sides together, aligning the raw edges as shown, above right. Sew ¼" from both sides of the drawn line. Cut along the line to yield two flying-geese units that

measure 3½" × 6½", including seam allowances. Repeat to make 144 flying-geese units.

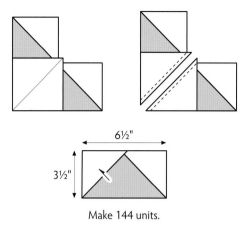

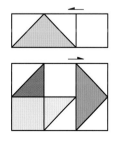

Make 144 units.

Making the A Blocks

For the scrappiest effect, mix as many different prints as possible in each block.

1. Lay out two half-square-triangle units, one print 3½" square, and one white 3½" square in two rows of two as shown. Join the units in each row, and then join the rows. Repeat to make 20 units measuring 6½" square, including seam allowances.

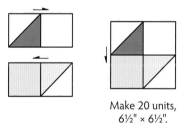

Make 20 units, 6½" × 6½".

2. Lay out one unit from step 1, two flying-geese units, and one white 3½" square in two rows as shown. Join the units in each row, and then join the rows. Repeat to make 20 units measuring 9½" square, including seam allowances.

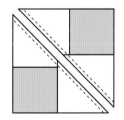 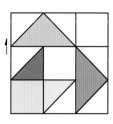

Make 20 units, 9½" × 9½".

3. Lay out a unit from step 2, two flying-geese units, and three white 3½" squares as shown. Join the side flying-geese unit and a white square into a column. Join the top flying-geese unit and two white squares into a row. Join the side column to the step 2 unit, and then join the rows. The completed unit should measure 12½" square, including seam allowances. Repeat to make 20 block units.

4. Lay out four step 3 units in two rows of two, orienting them to create the star design as shown. Join the units in each row, and then join the rows. The block should measure 24½" square, including seam allowances. Repeat to make five of block A.

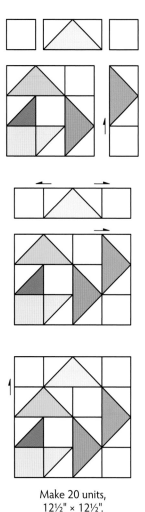

Make 20 units,
12½" × 12½".

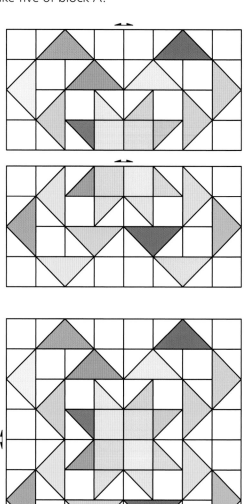

Make 5 of block A,
24½" × 24½".

Making the B Blocks

1. The block B units are constructed in the same manner as the block A units, but the placement of the print and white 3½" squares in two of the corners is reversed as shown. Make 16 block B units that measure 12½" square, including seam allowances.

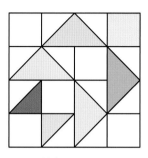

Make 16 units,
12½" × 12½".

2. Lay out four block B units in two rows of two, orienting them as shown. Join the units in each row, and then join the rows. The block should measure 24½" square, including seam allowances. Repeat to make four of block B.

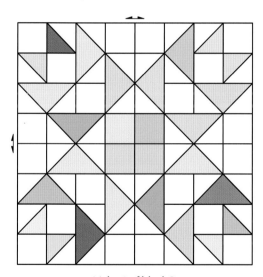

Make 4 of block B,
24½" × 24½".

Assembling the Quilt Top

1. Lay out the blocks in three rows of three, alternating them as shown in the quilt assembly diagram. Lay out the white 2½" × 24½" strips and the print 2½" squares around the blocks to create the sashing and cornerstones.

2. Join the horizontal sashing strips and cornerstones in each sashing row, and join the vertical sashing strips and blocks in each block row. Join the block rows and sashing rows. The finished quilt top should measure 80½" square.

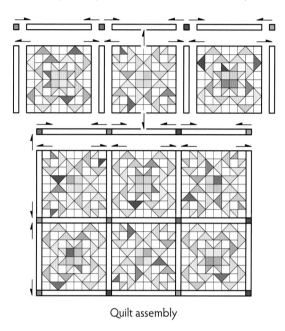

Quilt assembly

Finishing the Quilt

Go to ShopMartingale.com/HowtoQuilt for more details on quilting and finishing.

1. Layer the backing, batting, and quilt top; baste the layers together. Hand or machine quilt. The quilt shown is machine quilted with an allover starburst design.

2. Use the blue floral 2½"-wide strips to make the binding and then attach it to the quilt.

On Point

Six-pointed stars twinkle amidst darker diamonds, and you'll have a twinkle in your eye once you realize that triangles are all you need to create them.

Materials

Yardage is based on 42"-wide fabric.

3⅞ yards of white print for background and border
¼ yard *each* of 2 aqua and 2 pink prints for triangles
⅓ yard of black dot for triangles
¼ yard of black floral for triangles
12 strips, 2½" × 42", of assorted aqua, black, pink, and red prints for triangles
⅝ yard of aqua-and-white stripe for binding
4⅛ yards of fabric for backing
75" × 83" piece of batting
Equilateral triangle ruler (optional)

Cutting

All measurements include ¼" seam allowances.

From the white print, cut:
★ 28 strips, 4½" × 42"

From *each* aqua print, cut:
★ 2 strips, 4½" × 42" (4 total)

From *each* pink print, cut:
★ 2 strips, 4½" × 42" (4 total)

From the black dot, cut:
★ 2 strips, 4½" × 42"

From the black floral, cut:
★ 1 strip, 4½" × 42"

From the aqua-and-white stripe, cut:
★ 7 strips, 2¼" × 42"

Making the Triangles

Press all seam allowances as indicated by the arrows.

1. Sort the aqua, black, pink, and red 2½" strips into six pairs. Join each pair along the long edges. Each strip set should measure 4½" × 42".

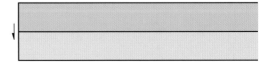

Make 6 strip sets,
4½" × 42".

On Point by Megan Jimenez; quilted by Rhonda Walker of Olie and Evie

FINISHED QUILT: 68½" × 72½"

2. The quilt is made entirely from equilateral triangles arranged in rows. To cut triangles from the strips, use the 4½" marking on a specialty equilateral triangle ruler, or make a template from the pattern on page 35. Place the ruler or template on one of the white 4½" strips as shown, and then rotary cut along the edges. Rotate the orientation of the ruler as you move along the strip, flipping it to cut each subsequent triangle.

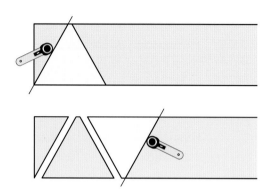

3. Cut the following numbers of triangles from the 4¼" strips and strip sets:

★ White print: 262 triangles total from 21 strips; reserve 7 strips for borders
★ Aqua prints: 18 triangles each (36 total)
★ Pink prints: 18 triangles each (36 total)
★ Strip sets: 12 triangles each (72 pieced triangles total)
★ Black dot: 18 triangles total
★ Black floral: 8 triangles total

Cut 262 triangles.

Cut 12 triangles from each strip set (72 total).

Cut 8 triangles.

Cut 18 triangles from each aqua (36 total).

Cut 18 triangles from each pink (36 total).

Cut 18 triangles.

Assembling the Quilt Top

1. Lay out the triangles in 16 rows of 27 triangles each, positioning them to create the star pattern as shown in the quilt assembly diagram below. Place the flat ends of the triangles along the upper and lower edges of the rows.

2. To join the triangles in each row, flip the triangle on the right on top of the triangle on the left and align the triangle tips so that the bottom triangle extends beyond the flat end on the top triangle. Sew the triangles together. Continue in the same way, adding one triangle at a time and alternating their orientation until the row is complete.

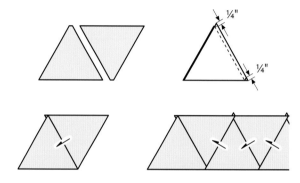

3. Sew the triangle rows together.

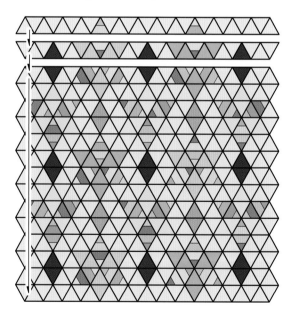

Quilt assembly

4. To square the uneven sides of the quilt, trim ¼" beyond the points of the outer triangles to account for ¼" seam allowance. The quilt top should measure approximately 60½" × 64½", including seam allowances.

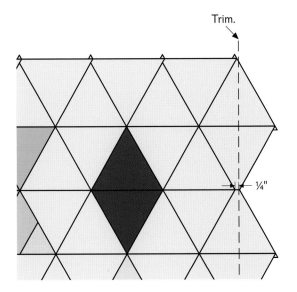

Trim.

¼"

5. Join the remaining white 4½"-wide strips end to end. From the pieced length, cut two strips, 66" long, for the side borders, and then trim them to fit your quilt top. Cut two strips, 68½" long, for the top and bottom borders. Sew the side borders to the quilt top first, and then trim the top and bottom borders to fit. The finished quilt top should measure 68½" × 72½".

Finishing the Quilt

Go to ShopMartingale.com/HowtoQuilt for more details on quilting and finishing.

1. Layer the backing, batting, and quilt top; baste the layers together. Hand or machine quilt. The quilt shown is machine quilted with an allover clamshell pattern.

2. Use the stripe 2½"-wide strips to make the binding and then attach it to the quilt.

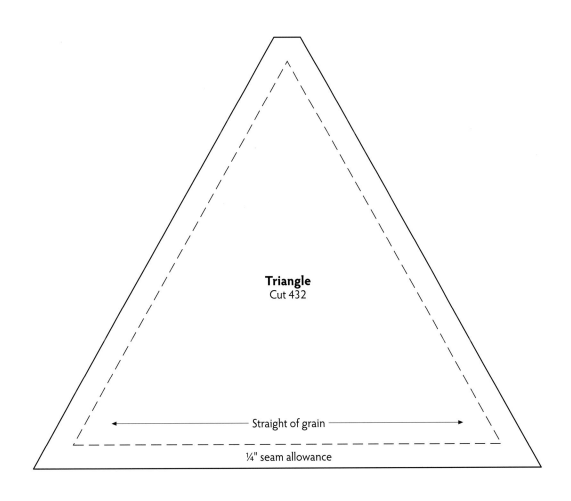

Triangle
Cut 432

Straight of grain

¼" seam allowance

Sprightly Stars

Turn your stash into stars! Start by choosing ten fat quarters, then set your sights on making a star attraction.

Materials

Yardage is based on 42"-wide fabric. Fat quarters measure 18" × 21"; each fat quarter yields 2 blocks.

10 fat quarters of assorted bright prints for blocks
1⅜ yards of navy stripe for blocks, middle border, and binding
2¾ yards of white dot for blocks and inner border
1⅞ yards of multicolored print for outer border
3¾ yards of fabric for backing
68" × 79" piece of batting

Cutting

All measurements include ¼" seam allowances.

From *each* of the 10 bright print fat quarters, cut:
★ 1 square, 4⅞" × 4⅞" (10 total)
★ 16 squares, 2½" × 2½" (160 total)
★ 8 squares, 2" × 2" (80 total)

From the navy stripe, cut:
★ 6 strips, 1½" × 42"
★ 4 strips, 1¾" × 42"; crosscut into 80 squares, 1¾" × 1¾"
★ 10 squares, 4⅞" × 4⅞"
★ 8 strips, 2½" × 42"

From the white dot, cut:
★ 6 strips, 2" × 42"
★ 14 strips, 2½" × 42"; crosscut into:
     80 rectangles, 2½" × 4½"
     80 squares, 2½" × 2½"
★ 80 strips, 2" × 8½"

From the *lengthwise* grain of the multicolored print, cut:
★ 2 strips, 5½" × 60½"
★ 2 strips, 5½" × 59½"

Sprightly Stars by Kimberly Jolly; pieced by Codi Mangrum; quilted by Diane Selman of mylongarm.com

FINISHED QUILT: 59½" × 70½"

FINISHED BLOCK: 11" × 11"

Making the Blocks

Press all seam allowances as indicated by the arrows.

1. Draw a diagonal line from corner to corner on the wrong side of the bright 4⅞" squares. Place one marked square and one navy 4⅞" square with right sides together. Sew ¼" from each side of the marked line. Cut the squares apart on the marked line to yield two half-square-triangle units that measure 4½" square, including seam allowances. Repeat to make 20 units.

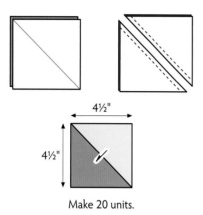

Make 20 units.

2. Draw a diagonal line from corner to corner on the wrong side of two matching bright 2½" squares. Place a marked square on one end of a white rectangle with right sides together, orienting the line as shown. Stitch on the marked line, and then trim the seam allowance to ¼". Repeat to add a matching bright square to the opposite end of the rectangle. The flying-geese unit should measure 2½" × 4½", including seam allowances. Make four.

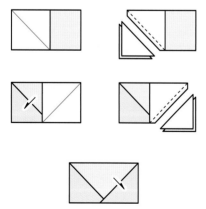

3. Draw a diagonal line from corner to corner on the wrong side of the navy 1¾" squares. Place a marked square on the bottom-right corner of the flying-geese unit with right sides together as shown. Stitch on the marked line, and then trim the seam allowance to ¼". Repeat to make four matching units that measure 2½" × 4½", including seam allowances.

Make 4 units,
2½" × 4½".

4. Lay out four white 2½" squares, the four matching flying-geese units, and a matching half-square-triangle unit in three rows as shown. Join the units in each row, and then join the rows. The block center should measure 8½" square, including seam allowances.

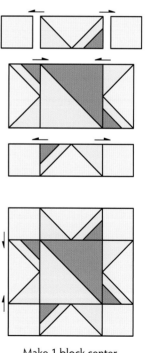

Make 1 block center,
8½" × 8½".

5. Lay out four matching bright 2" squares, four white 2" × 8½" strips, and the block center in three rows. Join the units in each row, and then join the rows. The Sprightly Star block should measure 11½" square, including seam allowances. Repeat to make 20 blocks.

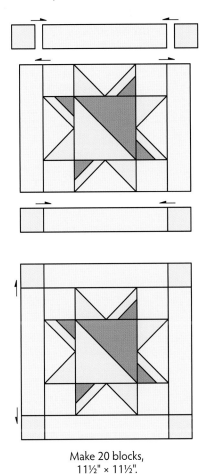

Make 20 blocks,
11½" × 11½".

Assembling the Quilt Top

1. Lay out the blocks in five rows of four, rotating them as shown in the quilt assembly diagram at right. Join the blocks in each row, and then join the rows. The quilt center should measure 44½" × 55½", including seam allowances.

2. Join the white 2"-wide strips end to end. From the pieced length, cut two strips, 55½" long, for the side borders and two strips, 47½" long, for the top and bottom borders. Sew the side borders to the quilt top first, and then add the top and bottom borders. The quilt top should measure 47½" × 58½", including seam allowances.

3. Join the navy 1½"-wide strips end to end. From the pieced length, cut two strips, 58½" long, for the side borders and two strips, 49½" long, for the top and bottom borders. Sew the side borders to the quilt top first, and then add the top and bottom borders. The quilt top should now measure 49½" × 60½", including seam allowances.

4. Sew the multicolored 60½"-long strips to the sides of the quilt center, and then add the multicolored 59½"-long strips to the top and bottom. The finished quilt top should measure 59½" × 70½".

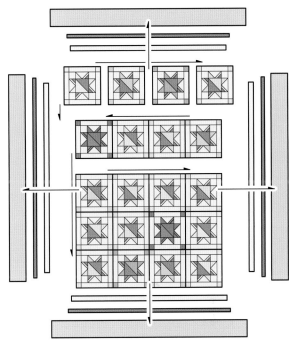

Quilt assembly

Finishing the Quilt

Go to ShopMartingale.com/HowtoQuilt for more details on quilting and finishing.

1. Layer the backing, batting, and quilt top; baste the layers together. Hand or machine quilt. The quilt shown is machine quilted with an allover circle pattern.

2. Use the navy 2½"-wide strips to make the binding and then attach it to the quilt.

Scrappy Stars

Sweet stars big and little dance across this fat quarter–friendly quilt. Mix soft pastel prints for a design that gently sparkles.

Materials

Yardage is based on 42"-wide fabric. Fat quarters measure 18" × 21".

20 to 28 fat quarters of assorted pastel prints for blocks*
4 yards of white solid for background
⅔ yard of apricot stripe for binding
7⅜ yards of fabric for backing
89" × 89" piece of batting

Use more fat quarters for greater variety.

Cutting

All measurements include ¼" seam allowances. The quilt consists of one extra-large 32" Star, four large 24" Stars, eight medium 16" Stars, and 16 small 8" Stars. Cut and sort the pieces for each Star block to keep them organized.

From the assorted fat quarters, cut the following pieces for each block size:

EXTRA-LARGE STAR
★ 4 matching squares, 8⅞" × 8⅞"
★ 4 matching squares, 4⅞" × 4⅞"
★ 4 assorted squares, 4½" × 4½"

LARGE STARS
★ 4 sets of 4 matching squares, 6⅞" × 6⅞" (16 total)
★ 16 assorted squares, 6½" × 6½"

MEDIUM STARS
★ 8 sets of 4 matching squares, 4⅞" × 4⅞" (32 total)
★ 8 assorted squares, 8½" × 8½", from the same prints as the 8 sets above

SMALL STARS
★ 16 sets of 4 matching squares, 2⅞" × 2⅞" (64 total)
★ 16 assorted squares, 4½" × 4½"

Continued on page 42

Scrappy Stars by Melissa Corry
FINISHED QUILT: 80½" × 80½"
FINISHED BLOCKS: 8", 16", 24", and 32" square

Continued from page 40

From the white solid, cut:

★ 1 square, 17¼" × 17¼"
★ 4 squares, 13¼" × 13¼"
★ 9 squares, 9¼" × 9¼"
★ 1 strip, 8½" × 42"; crosscut into 4 squares, 8½" × 8½"
★ 3 strips, 6½" × 42"; crosscut into 16 squares, 6½" × 6½"
★ 3 strips, 5¼" × 42"; crosscut into 16 squares, 5¼" × 5¼"
★ 4 strips, 4½" × 42"; crosscut into 36 squares, 4½" × 4½"
★ 4 strips, 2½" × 42"; crosscut into 64 squares, 2½" × 2½"

From the apricot stripe, cut:

★ 8 strips, 2½" × 42"

Making the Flying-Geese Units

Press all seam allowances as indicated by the arrows.

1. Starting with the print pieces designated for the Extra-Large Star block, place matching print 4⅞" squares on opposite corners of a white 9¼" square with right sides together, aligning the edges as shown. Draw a diagonal line from the top-left corner to the bottom-right corner. Sew ¼" from both sides of the drawn line. Cut along the drawn line to yield two units.

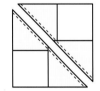

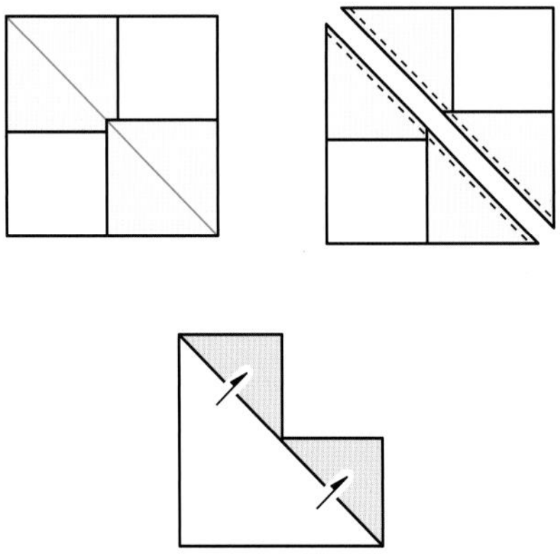

2. Draw a diagonal line from corner to corner on the wrong side of a matching print 4⅞" square. Place the marked square on the corner of one of the step 1 units with right sides together, aligning the raw edges as shown, above right. Sew ¼" from both sides of the drawn line. Cut along the line to yield two flying-geese

units that measure 4½" × 8½", including seam allowances. Repeat to make four units.

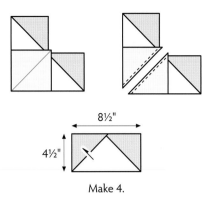

8½"

4½"

Make 4.

Making the Extra-Large Star Block

1. Lay out the four assorted print 4½" squares in two rows of two. Join the squares in each row, and then join the rows to create a four-patch unit that measures 8½" square, including seam allowances.

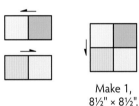

Make 1, 8½" × 8½".

2. Lay out the four flying-geese units, four white 4½" squares, and the four-patch unit in three rows as shown. Join the units in each row, and then join the rows to make the block center measuring 16½" square, including seam allowances.

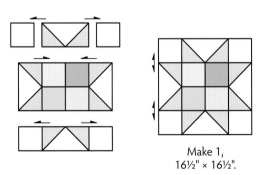

Make 1, 16½" × 16½".

3. Using four matching 8⅞" squares and one white 17¼" square, follow the method in "Making the Flying-Geese Units" at left to make four flying-geese units that measure 8½" × 16½", including seam allowances.

4. Lay out the four flying-geese units, four white 8½" squares, and the block center in three rows as shown. Join the units in each row, and then join the rows. The Extra-Large Star block should measure 32½" square, including seam allowances.

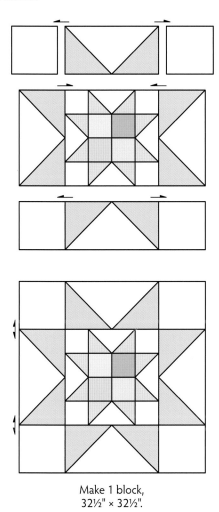

Make 1 block,
32½" × 32½".

Making the Large Star Blocks

1. Referring to step 1 of "Making the Extra-Large Star Block" on page 42, use four assorted 6½" squares to make a four-patch unit. The unit should measure 12½" square, including seam allowances.

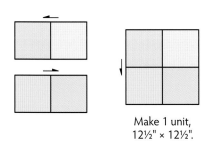

Make 1 unit,
12½" × 12½".

2. Using four matching 6⅞" squares and one white 13¼" square, follow the method in "Making the Flying-Geese Units" to make four flying-geese units that measure 6½" × 12½", including seam allowances.

3. Use the four-patch unit from step 1, the flying-geese units from step 2, and four white 6½" squares to make a Star block. The block should measure 24½" square, including seam allowances. Repeat to make four Large Star blocks.

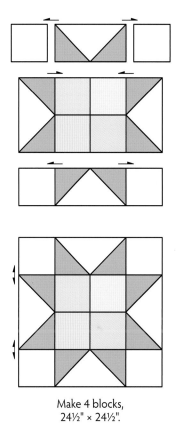

Make 4 blocks,
24½" × 24½".

Making the Medium Star Blocks

1. Using four matching 4⅞" squares and one white 9¼" square, follow the method in "Making the Flying-Geese Units" to make four flying-geese units that measure 4½" × 8½", including seam allowances.

2. Lay out the flying-geese units from step 1, four white 4½" squares, and a matching print 8½" square in three rows. Join the units in each row, and then join the rows. The block should measure 16½" square, including seam allowances. Repeat to make eight Medium Star blocks.

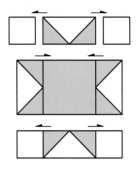
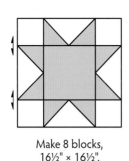

Make 8 blocks,
16½" × 16½".

Making the Small Star Blocks

1. Using four matching 2⅞" squares and one white 5¼" square, follow the method in "Making the Flying-Geese Units" to make four flying-geese units that measure 2½" × 4½", including seam allowances.

2. Lay out the four flying-geese units from step 1, four white 2½" squares, and a contrasting print 4½" square in three rows as shown. Join the units in each row, and then join the rows. The block should measure 8½" square, including seam allowances. Repeat to make 16 Small Star blocks.

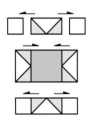

Make 16 blocks,
8½" × 8½".

Assembling the Six-Star Units

1. Lay out two Small Star blocks and one Medium Star block as shown. Sew the Small Star blocks together, and then join them to the Medium Star block. The unit should measure

16½" × 24½", including seam allowances. Make eight three-star units.

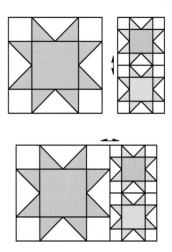

Make 8 units,
16½" × 24½".

2. Lay out two three-star units, alternating the placement of the Medium Star blocks as shown. Join the units. Repeat to make two units that measure 24½" × 32½", including seam allowances.

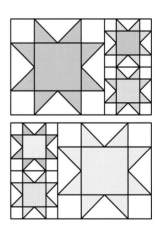

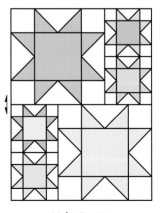

Make 2 units,
24½" × 32½".

3. Repeat step 2, but reverse the placement of the Medium Star blocks as shown. Make two units.

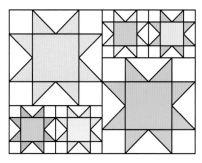

Make 2 units,
24½" × 32½".

Assembling the Quilt Top

1. Lay out the blocks and six-star units in three rows as shown in the quilt assembly diagram below.

2. Join the units in each row, and then join the rows. The finished quilt top should measure 80½" square.

Finishing the Quilt

Go to ShopMartingale.com/HowtoQuilt for more details on quilting and finishing.

1. Layer the backing, batting, and quilt top; baste the layers together. Hand or machine quilt. The quilt shown is machine quilted with an echoing orange peel pattern.

2. Use the apricot 2½"-wide strips to make the binding and then attach it to the quilt.

Quilt assembly

Star Candy

Make a sweet quilt featuring candy-color stars and stripes against a fresh white background. The blocks and sashing strips are easy to construct from half-square-triangle units.

Materials

Yardage is based on 42"-wide fabric.

⅝ yard of light blue solid for blocks and binding
¼ yard *each* of pink and green solid for blocks
⅛ yard *each* of dark blue, lavender, berry, yellow, and orange solid for blocks
2⅛ yards of white solid for background
3 yards of fabric for backing
55" × 55" piece of batting

Cutting

All measurements include ¼" seam allowances.

From the light blue solid, cut:
★ 8 squares, 3⅞" × 3⅞"
★ 5 strips, 2½" × 42"

From the pink solid, cut:
★ 2 strips, 3⅞" × 42"; crosscut into 16 squares, 3⅞" × 3⅞"

From the green solid, cut:
★ 2 strips, 3⅞" × 42"; crosscut into 11 squares, 3⅞" × 3⅞"

From *each* of the dark blue, lavender, berry, yellow, and orange solids, cut:
★ 8 squares, 3⅞" × 3⅞" (40 total)

From the white solid, cut:
★ 5 strips, 3⅞" × 42"; crosscut into 52 squares, 3⅞" × 3⅞"
★ 2 strips, 3½" × 42"; crosscut into 20 squares, 3½" × 3½"
★ 4 rectangles, 12½" × 15½"
★ 4 rectangles, 3½" × 15½"
★ 4 rectangles, 3½" × 12½"

Star Candy by Jackie White
FINISHED QUILT: 48½" × 48½"
FINISHED BLOCK: 12" × 12"

Making the Blocks

Press all seam allowances as indicated by the arrows.

1. Draw a diagonal line from corner to corner on the wrong side of three light blue squares. Place a marked square right sides together with a dark blue square. Sew ¼" from both sides of the drawn line. Cut along the drawn line to yield two half-square-triangle units. Trim the unit to measure 3½" square, including seam allowances. Repeat to make six light blue/dark blue units (one is extra).

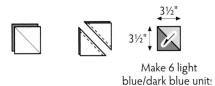

Make 6 light blue/dark blue units

2. Repeat the process from step 1 to make five orange/green units, five pink/purple units, and five yellow/berry units.

Make 5 orange/green units.

Make 5 pink/lavender units.

Make 5 berry/yellow units.

3. Draw a diagonal line from corner to corner on the wrong side of the white 3⅞" squares. Repeat the process from step 1 to make the following units:

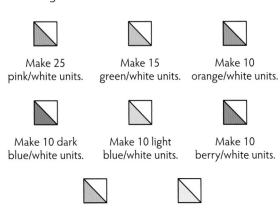

Make 25 pink/white units.

Make 15 green/white units.

Make 10 orange/white units.

Make 10 dark blue/white units.

Make 10 light blue/white units.

Make 10 berry/white units.

Make 10 lavender/white units.

Make 10 yellow/white units.

4. Lay out four white 3½" squares and one half-square-triangle unit of each color combination in four rows of four as shown, matching the colors to create a star pattern. Join the units in each row, and then join the rows. The block should measure 12½" square, including seam allowances. Repeat to make five blocks.

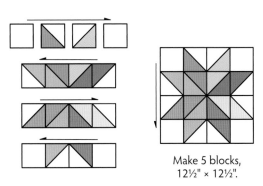

Make 5 blocks, 12½" × 12½".

5. Sew white 3½" × 12½" rectangles to the right edge of two blocks. Sew white 3½" × 12½" rectangles to the left edge of two blocks. The blocks should measure 12½" × 15½", including seam allowances.

6. Sew a white 3½" × 15½" rectangle to the top of one block with a right-side strip. Sew an identical rectangle to the top of one block with a left-side strip. Sew the remaining white 3½" × 15½" rectangles to the bottom of the remaining blocks with side strips.

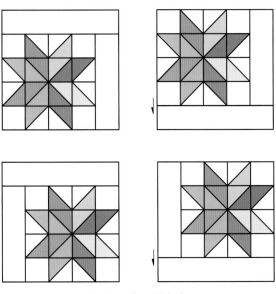

Make 1 of each block, 15½" × 15½".

Making the Sashing Strips

1. Join five green/white half-square-triangle units in a row, orienting the units as shown. Repeat to make two green/white pieced sashing strips that measure 3½" × 15½", including seam allowances.

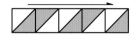

Make 2 strips,
3½" × 15½".

2. In the same manner as step 1, make one pieced sashing strip in each of the following combinations: yellow/white, lavender/white, dark blue/white, light blue/white, orange/white, and berry/white. Carefully position the half-square-triangle units as shown to create the striped effect.

Make 1 yellow/white unit.

Make 1 light blue/white unit.

Make 1 lavender/white unit.

Make 1 orange/white unit.

Make 1 dark blue/white unit.

Make 1 berry/white unit.

3. Join four pink/white half-square-triangle units as shown to make a sashing strip that measures 3½" × 12½", including seam allowances. Make two strips.

Make 2 strips,
3½" × 12½".

4. Join the 12 remaining pink/white units as shown into two sashing strips of six units each that measure 3½" × 18½", including seam allowances.

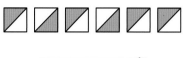

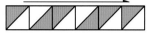

Make 2 strips,
3½" × 18½".

Assembling the Quilt Top

Lay out the blocks, sashing strips, and white 12½" × 15½" rectangles in five columns as shown in the quilt assembly diagram. Join the pieces in each column, and then join the columns. The finished quilt top should measure 48½" square.

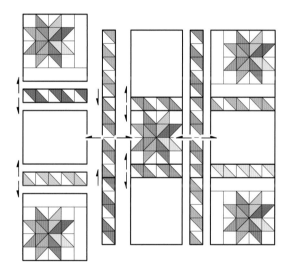

Quilt assembly

Finishing the Quilt

Go to ShopMartingale.com/HowtoQuilt for more details on quilting and finishing.

1. Layer the backing, batting, and quilt top; baste the layers together. Hand or machine quilt. The quilt shown is machine quilted with an echoing diamond pattern in each Star block and stripes of stippling in the background.

2. Use the light blue 2½"-wide strips to make the binding and then attach it to the quilt.

Hazelwood Stars

By rotating these striking blocks throughout the quilt, Krystal created a secondary pattern of interlocking white chevrons, adding movement to the design. For a super scrappy effect, use a fat quarter in a different print for each block.

Materials

Yardage is based on 42"-wide fabric. Fat quarters measure 18" × 21".

36 fat eighths or fat quarters of assorted bright prints for blocks*
4⅝ yards of white tone on tone for blocks and border
⅝ yard of aqua dot for binding
4⅛ yards of fabric for backing
74" × 74" piece of batting

A fat eighth (9" × 21") is sufficient if you cut carefully.

Cutting

All measurements include ¼" seam allowances. Group the matching pieces from each fat quarter together, as one block is made from each print.

From *each* of the 36 bright prints, cut:*
★ 2 squares, 3⅜" × 3⅜" (72 total)
★ 2 rectangles, 3" × 5½" (72 total)
★ 8 squares, 3" × 3" (288 total)

See diagram below.

From the *lengthwise* grain of the white tone on tone, cut:
★ 2 strips, 3" × 65½"
★ 2 strips, 3" × 60½"
★ 4 strips, 3⅜" × 65"; crosscut into 72 squares, 3⅜" × 3⅜"
★ 2 strips, 5½" × 65"; crosscut into 22 squares, 5½" × 5½"

From the remainder of the white tone on tone, cut:
★ 2 strips, 5½" × 42"; crosscut into 14 squares, 5½" × 5½"
★ 23 strips, 3" × 42"; crosscut into:
    72 rectangles, 3" × 5½"
    144 squares, 3" × 3"

From the aqua dot, cut:
★ 8 strips, 2½" × 42"

Cutting from a fat eighth

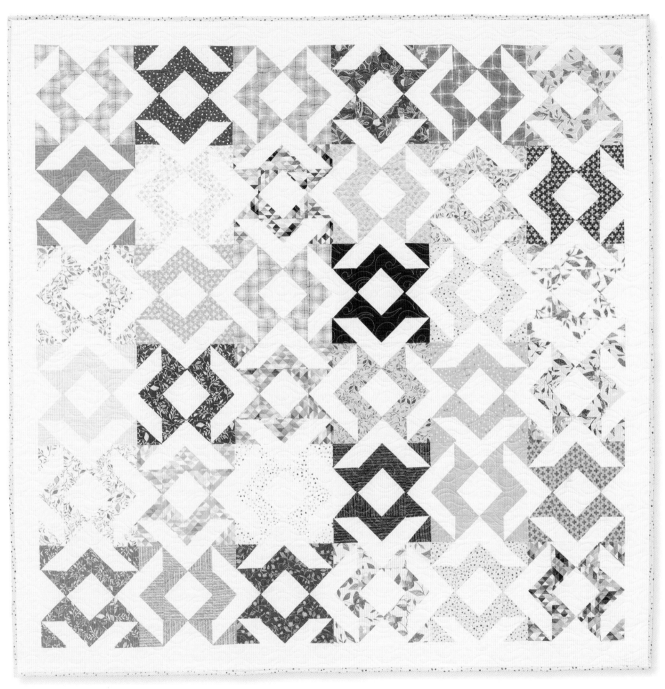

Hazelwood Stars by Krystal Stahl; quilted by Diane Selman of mylongarm.com

FINISHED QUILT: 65½" × 65½"

FINISHED BLOCK: 10" × 10"

Making the Blocks

Use matching print pieces for each block. Press all seam allowances as indicated by the arrows.

1. Draw a diagonal line from corner to corner on the wrong side of four matching print 3" squares. Place the marked squares on opposite corners of a white 5½" square with right sides together as shown. Sew on the marked lines. Trim ¼" from each seam and press. Sew the remaining marked squares to the remaining corners in the same manner. The block center should measure 5½" square, including seam allowances.

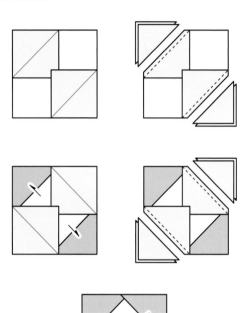

Make 1 block center,
5½" × 5½".

2. Draw a diagonal line from corner to corner on the wrong side of a white 3⅜" square. Layer the marked square right sides together with a print 3⅜" square. Sew ¼" from each side of the marked line. Cut the squares apart on the marked line to yield two half-square-triangle units. Trim the units to measure 3" square, including seam allowances. Repeat to make four units.

Make 4 units.

3. Draw a diagonal line from corner to corner on the wrong side of four matching print 3" squares. Place a marked square right sides together on one end of a white 3" × 5½" rectangle as shown. Stitch on the marked line. Trim ¼" from the seam. Repeat to add a matching print square to the opposite end of the rectangle. The flying-geese unit should measure 3" × 5½", including seam allowances. Make two. In the same manner, make two flying-geese units using white 3" squares and print 3" × 5½" rectangles.

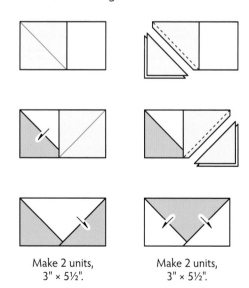

Make 2 units,   Make 2 units,
3" × 5½".   3" × 5½".

4. Lay out the four half-square-triangle units, the four flying-geese units, and the block center in three rows as shown. Join the units into rows, and then join the rows. The block should measure 10½" square, including seam allowances. Repeat with each set of matching print pieces to make 36 blocks.

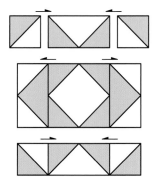
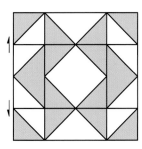

Make 36 blocks,
10½" × 10½".

Assembling the Quilt Top

1. Lay out the blocks in six rows of six, rotating alternate blocks a quarter turn as shown in the quilt assembly diagram. Join the blocks in each row, and then join the rows. The quilt center should measure 60½" square, including seam allowances.

2. Sew the white 60½"-long strips to the sides of the quilt center, and then add the white 65½"-long strips to the top and bottom. The finished quilt top should measure 65½" square.

Finishing the Quilt

Go to ShopMartingale.com/HowtoQuilt for more details on quilting and finishing.

1. Layer the backing, batting, and quilt top; baste the layers together. Hand or machine quilt. The quilt shown is machine quilted with an allover swirl design.

2. Use the aqua 2½"-wide strips to make the binding and then attach it to the quilt.

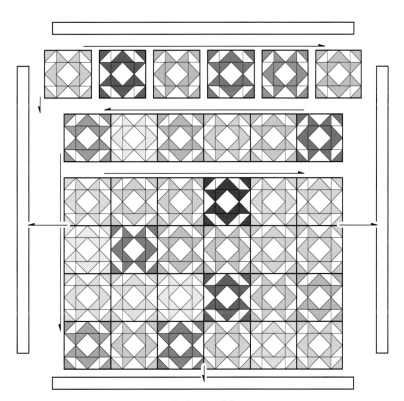

Quilt assembly

Dazzling Stars

These intricate Star blocks are actually made with simple patchwork techniques. The added touch of an appliquéd circle in the center of each block lends personality and focus to the design.

Materials
Yardage is based on 42"-wide fabric.

2⅝ yards of aqua dot for blocks and binding
1⅝ yards of cream solid for blocks
1⅛ yard of black dot for blocks
¼ yard of white solid for appliqué circles
3 yards of fabric for backing
54" × 54" piece of batting
Supplies for your favorite appliqué method

Cutting
All measurements include ¼" seam allowances.

From the aqua dot, cut:
★ 23 strips, 2½" × 42"; crosscut *17 strips* into:
    96 rectangles, 2½" × 4½"
    96 squares, 2½" × 2½"
★ 3 strips, 4½" × 42"; crosscut into:
    8 rectangles, 4½" × 8½"
    8 squares, 4½" × 4½"
★ 2 strips, 2⅞" × 42"; crosscut into 24 squares, 2⅞" × 2⅞"
★ 2 squares, 4⅞" × 4⅞"

From the cream solid, cut:
★ 2 strips, 4½" × 42"; crosscut into:
    4 rectangles, 4½" × 8½"
    8 squares, 4½" × 4½"
★ 2 strips, 2⅞" × 42"; crosscut into 24 squares, 2⅞" × 2⅞"
★ 12 strips, 2½" × 42"; crosscut into:
    48 rectangles, 2½" × 4½"
    96 squares, 2½" × 2½"
★ 2 squares, 4⅞" × 4⅞"

From the black dot, cut:
★ 1 square, 8½" × 8½"
★ 3 strips, 4½" × 42"; crosscut into 20 squares, 4½" × 4½"
★ 6 strips, 2½" × 42"; crosscut into 96 squares, 2½" × 2½"

Dazzling Stars by Kimberly Jolly; pieced by Elva Curtis; quilted by Diane Selman of mylongarm.com

FINISHED QUILT: 48½" × 48½"

FINISHED BLOCKS: 24" × 24" and 12" × 12"

Making the Blocks

Press all seam allowances as indicated by the arrows.

1. Draw a diagonal line from corner to corner on the wrong side of a cream 4⅞" square. Place the marked square right sides together with an aqua 4⅞" square. Sew ¼" from both sides of the marked line. Cut along the line to yield two half-square-triangle units. The units should measure 4½" square, including seam allowances. Repeat to make four. Using the same technique with the cream and aqua 2⅞" squares, make 48 small half-square-triangle units that measure 2½" square, including seam allowances.

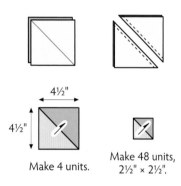

4½"

4½"

Make 4 units.

Make 48 units, 2½" × 2½".

2. Draw a diagonal line from corner to corner on the wrong side of a cream 4½" square. Place the marked square right sides together on one end of an aqua 4½" × 8½" rectangle as shown. Sew on the marked line. Trim ¼" from the seam. Make four folded-corner units. Using the same technique with cream 2½" squares and aqua 2½" × 4½" rectangles, make 48 small folded-corner units.

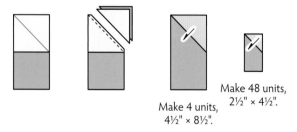

Make 4 units, 4½" × 8½".

Make 48 units, 2½" × 4½".

3. Lay out a cream 4½" square, a large half-square-triangle unit, and a large folded-corner unit as shown above right. Join the square and half-square-triangle unit, and then add the folded-

corner unit. Make four units that measure 8½" square, including seam allowances. Using the same technique and the small half-square-triangle units, folded-corner units, and cream 2½" squares, make 48 small pieced squares that measure 4½" square, including seam allowances.

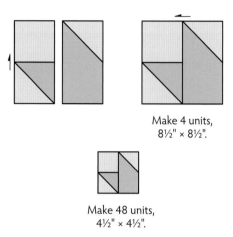

Make 4 units, 8½" × 8½".

Make 48 units, 4½" × 4½".

4. Draw a diagonal line from corner to corner on the wrong side of two aqua 4½" squares. Place a marked square right sides together on one end of a cream 4½" × 8½" rectangle as shown. Stitch on the marked line. Trim ¼" from the seam. Repeat to add the second marked square to the opposite end of the rectangle. The large cream/aqua flying-geese unit should measure 4½" × 8½", including seam allowances. Make four. In the same manner, make 48 small cream/aqua flying-geese units using aqua 2½" squares and cream 2½" × 4½" rectangles.

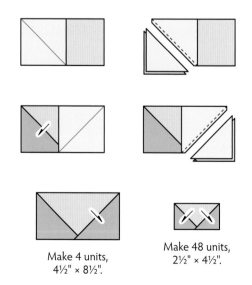

Make 4 units, 4½" × 8½".

Make 48 units, 2½" × 4½".

5. Repeat the process from step 4 to make four large black/aqua flying-geese units and 48 small black/aqua flying-geese units.

Make 4 units,
4½" × 8½".

Make 48 units,
2½" × 4½".

6. Lay out one large cream/aqua flying-geese unit and one large black/aqua flying-geese unit as shown. Join the units. Repeat to make four flying-geese squares that measure 8½" square, including seam allowances. In the same manner, use the small flying-geese units to make 48 small flying-geese squares that measure 4½" square, including seam allowances.

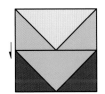

Make 4 units,
8½" × 8½".

Make 48 units,
4½" × 4½".

7. Using your favorite appliqué method and the patterns on page 58, prepare one large circle and 12 small circles from the white solid. Appliqué the large circle to the center of the black 8½" square. Appliqué a small circle to the center of each of the remaining black 4½" squares.

8. Lay out the four large pieced squares, four large flying-geese squares, and the appliquéd 8½" square in three rows as shown. Join the units in each row, and then join the rows. The large block should measure 24½" square, including seam allowances.

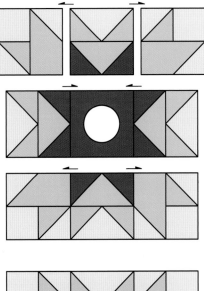

Make 1 large block,
24½" × 24½".

9. In the same manner as step 8, lay out four small pieced squares, four small flying-geese squares, and one appliquéd 4½" square in three rows as shown. Join the units in each row, and then join the rows. Make 12 small blocks that measure 12½" square, including seam allowances.

Make 12 small blocks,
12½" × 12½".

Assembling the Quilt Top

1. Lay out the large and small blocks in three rows as shown in the quilt assembly diagram, at right. Join the small blocks on each side of the center row into two units, and then sew the units to opposite sides of the large block.

2. Join the small blocks in the top and bottom rows, and then sew these rows to the center row. The finished quilt top should measure 48½" square.

Finishing the Quilt

Go to ShopMartingale.com/HowtoQuilt for more details on quilting and finishing.

1. Layer the backing, batting, and quilt top; baste the layers together. Hand or machine quilt. The quilt shown is machine quilted with an allover swirl and feather design.

2. Use the remaining aqua 2½"-wide strips to make the binding and then attach it to the quilt.

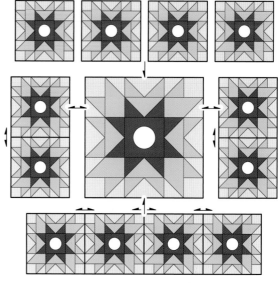

Quilt assembly

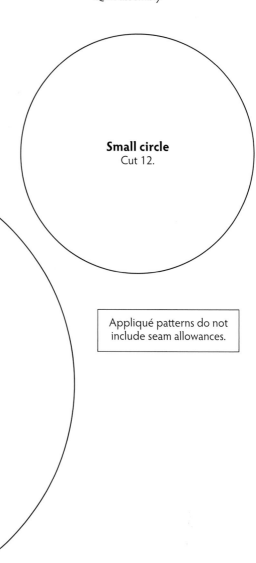

Small circle
Cut 12.

Appliqué patterns do not include seam allowances.

Large circle
Cut 1.

Ties That Bind

Materials

Yardage is based on 42"-wide fabric. Fat quarters measure 18" × 21"; fat eighths are 9" × 21".

15 fat quarters of assorted light prints for block backgrounds and scrappy inner border

47 fat eighths of assorted medium and dark prints for blocks

1¼ yards of green paisley for outer border

¾ yard of red print for binding

7½ yards of fabric for backing

90" × 90" piece of batting

Cutting

All measurements include ¼" seam allowances.

From the light prints, cut a *total* of:
★ 50 squares, 4⅞" × 4⅞"; cut the squares in half diagonally to yield 100 triangles
★ 150 squares, 2⅞" × 2⅞"; cut the squares in half diagonally to yield 300 triangles
★ 100 squares, 2½" × 2½"
★ 14 strips, 2½" × 21"

From the medium and dark prints, cut a *total* of:
★ 150 squares, 4⅞" × 4⅞"; cut the squares in half diagonally to yield 300 triangles
★ 150 squares, 2⅞" × 2⅞"; cut the squares in half diagonally to yield 300 triangles
★ 64 squares, 2½" × 2½"

From the green paisley, cut:
★ 8 strips, 4½" × 42"

From the red print, cut:
★ 9 strips, 2½" × 42"

Janet's family loves to vacation at the lake, so she chose colors based on good memories of playing in the hot summer sun; napping in the shade of the tall pine trees; and the daily treat of watching the magnificent sunsets as the sun slowly winks out across the lake each night.

Ties That Bind by Janet Rae Nesbitt; pieced by Sandi McKell; quilted by Kathy Woods

FINISHED QUILT: 80⅝" × 80⅝"

FINISHED BLOCK: 13⅝" × 13⅝"

Making the Blocks

Press all seam allowances as indicated by the arrows.

1. With right sides together, sew light and dark 2⅞" triangles together along their long edges to make 300 half-square-triangle units. Press the seam allowances toward the dark triangles. Make 300 units that measure 2½" square.

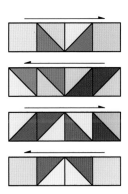

Make 300 units, 2½" × 2½".

2. Using four pairs of matching dark triangles for the star points, lay out 12 half-square-triangle units and four light 2½" squares as shown. Sew the pieces together in rows. Press the seam allowances in opposite directions from row to row. Join the rows and press the seam allowances in one direction. The block should measure 8½" square, including seam allowances. Make a total of 25 Star blocks.

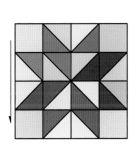

Make 25 blocks, 8½" × 8½".

3. With right sides together, sew light and dark 4⅞" triangles together along their long edges to make 100 half-square-triangle units. Press the seam allowances toward the dark triangles. Make 100 units that measure 4½" square.

Make 100 units, 4½" × 4½".

4. Lay out a half-square-triangle unit from step 3 and two dark 4⅞" triangles as shown. Join the pieces and press the seam allowances as indicated. Make a total of 100 lattice units.

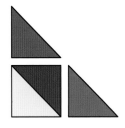 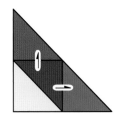

Make 100.

5. Sew lattice units to opposite sides of a Star block, aligning the point of the half-square-triangle units with the center seam of the block. Press the seam allowances as indicated. Trim the lattice units even with the edges of the block.

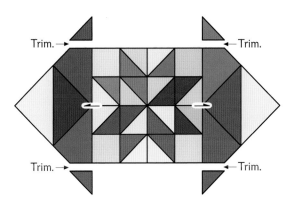

6. Add lattice units to the remaining two sides of the Star block, again aligning the point of the half-square-triangle units with the center seam of the block. Press. The block should measure 14⅛" square, including seam allowances.

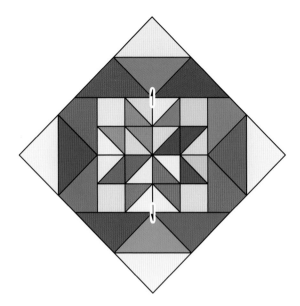

7. Place a dark 2½" square on one corner of the block, right sides together. Sew diagonally from corner to corner as shown. Trim the excess corner fabric ¼" from the sewn line. Press the seam allowances toward the resulting triangle. In the same manner, sew dark 2½" squares on the remaining three corners of the block. Make a total of nine blocks for the quilt center.

Make 9 blocks,
14⅛" × 14⅛".

8. To make the edge blocks, repeat steps 5 and 6 to make 12 blocks. Then place a dark 2½" square on *two* adjacent corners of each block. Sew diagonally from corner to corner as shown. Trim the excess corner fabric ¼" from the sewn line. Press the seam allowances toward the resulting triangle. Make six of each.

 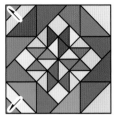

Make 6 of each block,
14⅛" × 14⅛".

9. To make the corner blocks, repeat steps 5 and 6 to make four blocks. Then place a dark 2½" square on *one* corner of each block. Sew diagonally from corner to corner as shown. Trim the excess corner fabric ¼" from the sewn line. Press the seam allowances toward the resulting triangle. Make four.

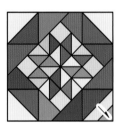

Make 4 blocks,
14⅛" × 14⅛".

Assembling the Quilt Top

1. Lay out the blocks in five rows of five as shown in the quilt assembly diagram on page 63. Sew the blocks together in rows. Press the seam allowances in opposite directions from row to row. Join the rows. Press the seam allowances in one direction. The quilt center should measure 68⅝" square.

2. Join the light 2½"-wide strips end to end. From the pieced strip, cut two strips, 68⅝" long, for the side borders and two strips, 72⅝" long, for the top and bottom borders. Sew the side borders to the quilt top first, and then add the top and bottom borders. Press all seam allowances toward the inner border.

3. Join the green paisley 4½"-wide strips end to end. From the pieced strip, cut two strips, 72⅝" long, for the side borders and two strips, 80⅝" long, for the top and bottom borders. Sew the side borders to the quilt top first, and then add the top and bottom borders. Press all seam allowances toward the outer border. The finished quilt top should measure 80⅝" square.

Finishing the Quilt

Go to ShopMartingale.com/HowtoQuilt for more details on quilting and finishing.

1. Layer the quilt top with batting and backing; baste. Hand or machine quilt. The quilt shown is machine quilted with swirls in the stars and feathers in the light border.

2. Use the red 2½"-wide strips to make the binding and then attach it to the quilt.

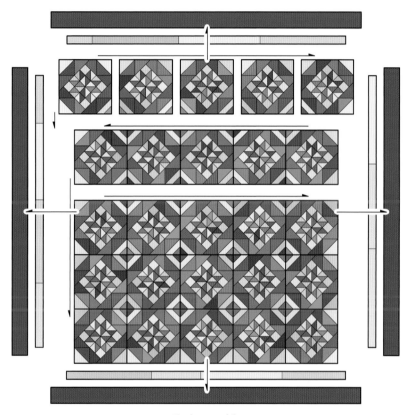

Quilt assembly

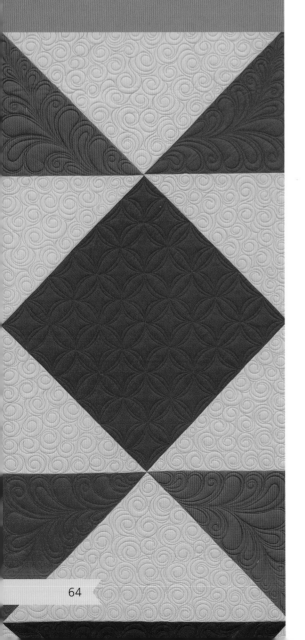

Big Star

Select your favorite color combination for a modern, graphic quilt featuring one giant star. The large open areas provide a great canvas for showing off distinctive free-motion quilting designs as Vicki did.

Materials

Yardage is based on 42"-wide fabric. Fat quarters measure 18" × 21".

9 fat quarters of assorted purple solids for blocks
3¾ yards of gray solid for background and binding
4 yards of fabric for backing
72" × 72" piece of batting

Cutting

All measurements include ¼" seam allowances.

From the purple fat quarters, cut a *total* of:
★ 4 squares, 17" × 17"
★ 1 square, 15½" × 15½"
★ 4 rectangles, 9" × 15½"

From the gray solid, cut:
★ 4 squares, 17" × 17"
★ 4 squares, 15½" × 15½"
★ 2 squares, 22½" × 22½"; cut the squares into quarters diagonally to yield 8 triangles
★ 2 squares, 11½" × 11½"; cut the squares in half diagonally to yield 4 triangles
★ 7 strips, 2½" × 42"

Making the Blocks

For the most interesting layout, mix up the shades of purple as much as possible when assembling the blocks. Press all seam allowances in the directions indicated by the arrows.

1. Draw a diagonal line from corner to corner on the wrong side of the gray 17" squares. Place a marked square on a purple 17" square, right sides together. Sew ¼" from both sides of

Big Star by Vicki Ruebel

FINISHED QUILT: 64" × 64"
FINISHED BLOCK: 15" × 15"

the drawn line. Cut along the line to yield two half-square-triangle units. Repeat to make eight units.

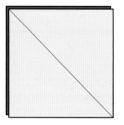 

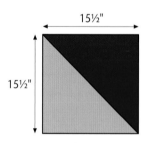

Make 8 units,
16⅝" × 16⅝".

2. Select four half-square-triangle units in different shades of purple and trim them to measure 15½" square. Set these units aside for quilt-top assembly.

Make 4 units.

3. Pair the remaining four half-square-triangle units. Layer the units in one pair right sides together, positioning the purple sections opposite each other and nesting the seam allowances. Draw a diagonal line perpendicular to the seam on the wrong side of the top unit. Sew ¼" from both sides of the line. Cut along the line to yield two Hourglass blocks. Repeat

for a total of four Hourglass blocks. Trim the blocks to measure 15½" square.

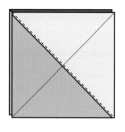 

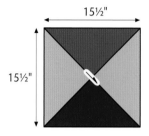

Make 4 blocks.

SQUARING UP

When trimming the Hourglass blocks, make sure to place the diagonal line of your ruler so that the ruler's 7¾" mark lines up with the exact center of the unit.

4. Place two purple 9" × 15½" rectangles right sides together. Mark the top edge of the pair ½" from the top-left corner and mark the bottom edge ½" from the bottom-right corner. Draw a line connecting the dots, and then cut along the line to yield four triangles. Repeat with the remaining purple rectangles for a total of eight triangles.

½"

½"   Cut 8 traingles.

5. Find the center point of the top edge of one gray 15½" square, and then mark ¼" down from the center. Draw a line from the mark to each lower corner of the square. Trim the square ¼" beyond both lines to yield a triangle. (Discard the trimmed outer pieces or add them to your scrap bin.) Repeat to cut four gray triangles.

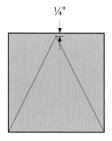

Cut 4 traingles.

6. Place one purple triangle from step 4 on one gray triangle with right sides together, aligning the long edge. Sew the edges.

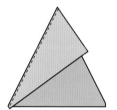
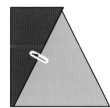

7. Repeat to sew a triangle in a different shade of purple to the opposite long edge of the gray triangle. Making sure the upper point of the triangle is centered, trim the block to measure 15½" square, including seam allowances. Repeat to make four Triangle blocks.

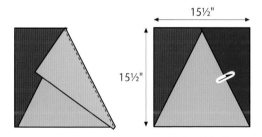

Make 4 blocks.

Assembling the Quilt Top

Lay out the blocks, the trimmed half-square-triangle units, the purple 15½" square, and the gray setting triangles in five diagonal rows as shown. Join the blocks and triangles in each row, and then join the rows. Add the corner triangles last. The finished quilt top should measure approximately 64" square.

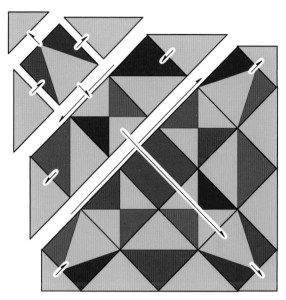

Quilt assembly

Finishing the Quilt

Go to ShopMartingale.com/HowtoQuilt for more details on quilting and finishing.

1. Layer the backing, batting, and quilt top; baste the layers together. Hand or machine quilt. The quilt shown is machine quilted with feathers in the purple triangles, an orange peel design in the center square, and a swirl motif in the background.

2. Use the gray 2½"-wide strips to make the binding and then attach it to the quilt.

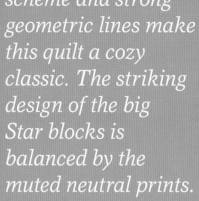

Dashing Stars

A sophisticated color scheme and strong geometric lines make this quilt a cozy classic. The striking design of the big Star blocks is balanced by the muted neutral prints.

Materials

Yardage is based on 42"-wide fabric.

1¾ yards of light taupe floral for blocks and binding
1½ yards of white dot for blocks
1⅜ yards of dark taupe dot for sashing and border
1 yard of dark taupe floral for blocks
1 yard of yellow floral for blocks and sashing squares
3⅞ yards of fabric for backing
69" × 69" piece of batting

Cutting

All measurements include ¼" seam allowances.

From the light taupe floral, cut:
★ 19 strips, 2½" × 42"; crosscut *12 strips* into 180 squares, 2½" × 2½"
★ 3 strips, 2⅞" × 42"; crosscut into 36 squares, 2⅞" × 2⅞"

From the white dot, cut:
★ 3 strips, 2⅞" × 42"; crosscut into 36 squares, 2⅞" × 2⅞"
★ 5 strips, 4½" × 42"; crosscut into 72 rectangles, 2½" × 4½"
★ 7 strips, 2½" × 42"; crosscut into 108 squares, 2½" × 2½"

From the dark taupe dot, cut:
★ 12 strips, 3½" × 16½"
★ 6 strips, 3½" × 42"

From the dark taupe floral, cut:
★ 9 squares, 4½" × 4½"
★ 6 strips, 2⅞" × 42"; crosscut into 72 squares, 2⅞" × 2⅞"
★ 3 strips, 2½" × 42"; crosscut into 36 squares, 2½" × 2½"

From the yellow floral, cut:
★ 3 strips, 4½" × 42"; crosscut into 36 rectangles, 2½" × 4½"
★ 5 strips, 2½" × 42"; crosscut into 72 squares, 2½" × 2½"
★ 4 squares, 3½" × 3½"

Dashing Stars by Kimberly Jolly; pieced by Melissa Garibay; quilted by Diane Selman of mylongarm.com

FINISHED QUILT: 60½" × 60½"

FINISHED BLOCK: 16" × 16"

Making the Blocks

Press all seam allowances as indicated by the arrows.

1. Draw a diagonal line from corner to corner on the wrong side of the white 2⅞" squares. Place a marked square right sides together with a dark taupe floral 2⅞" square. Sew ¼" from both sides of the marked line. Cut along the line to yield two half-square-triangle units. Repeat to make 72 units that measure 2½" square, including seam allowances.

Make 72 units,
2½" × 2½".

2. In the same manner as step 1, make 72 half-square-triangle units from the light and dark taupe floral 2⅞" squares.

Make 72 units,
2½" × 2½".

3. Draw a diagonal line from corner to corner on the wrong side of two light taupe 2½" squares. Place a marked square right sides together on one end of a white rectangle as shown. Stitch on the marked line. Trim ¼" from the seam and press. In the same manner, add the second marked square to the opposite end of the rectangle to make a flying-geese unit. Make 72 units measuring 2½" × 4½", including seam allowances.

Make 72 units,
2½" × 4½".

4. In the same manner as step 3, make 36 flying-geese units from white 2½" squares and yellow rectangles.

Make 36 units,
2½" × 4½".

5. Lay out one 2½" square each of white, light taupe, and dark taupe; two yellow 2½" squares; and two each of white/taupe and light/dark taupe half-square-triangle units in three rows as shown. Join the units in each row, and then join the rows. The unit should measure 6½" square, including seam allowances. Repeat to make 36 corner units.

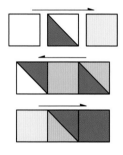 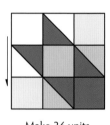

Make 36 units,
6½" × 6½".

6. Lay out two white/taupe flying-geese units and one white/yellow flying-geese unit in a column as shown. Join the units along the long edges. The unit should measure 4½" × 6½", including seam allowances. Repeat to make 36 side units.

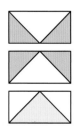 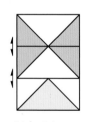

Make 36 units,
4½" × 6½".

7. Lay out four corner units, four side units, and one dark taupe floral 4½" square in three rows as shown. Join the units in each row, and then join the rows. Make nine blocks that measure 16½" square, including seam allowances.

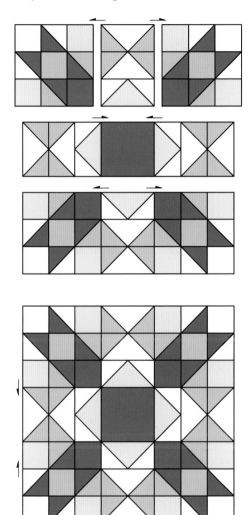

Make 9 blocks,
16½" × 16½".

Assembling the Quilt Top

1. Lay out the blocks in three rows of three, alternating them with dark taupe dot 3½" × 16½" strips as shown in the quilt assembly diagram. Lay out two sashing rows of three 16½" strips alternating with two yellow 3½" squares each as shown. Join the units in each row, and then join the rows. The quilt center should now measure 54½" square, including seam allowances.

2. Join the six dark taupe dot 42"-long strips end to end. From the pieced length, cut two strips, 54½" long, for the side borders and two strips, 60½" long, for the top and bottom borders. Sew the side borders to the quilt top first, and then add the top and bottom borders. The finished quilt top should measure 60½" square.

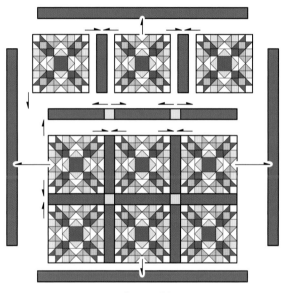

Quilt assembly

Finishing the Quilt

Go to ShopMartingale.com/HowtoQuilt for more details on quilting and finishing.

1. Layer the backing, batting, and quilt top; baste the layers together. Hand or machine quilt. The quilt shown is machine quilted with feathers in the border and an allover swirl and feather pattern in the blocks.

2. Use the remaining light taupe 2½"-wide strips to make the binding and then attach it to the quilt.

Hunter Star

The Hunter Star is a classic block with a striking eight-point design. Melissa's simple method for piecing the blocks uses just squares and half-square triangles.

Materials

Yardage is based on 42"-wide fabric. Fat quarters measure 18" × 21".

24 fat quarters of assorted bright prints for blocks
5 yards of white solid for background
⅞ yard of blue print for binding
8¾ yards of fabric for backing
104" × 104" piece of batting

Cutting

All measurements include ¼ seam allowances.

From *each* of 12 bright print fat quarters, cut:
★ 1 square, 8½" × 8½" (12 total)
★ 7 squares, 5" × 5" (84 total)

From *each* of the remaining 12 bright print fat quarters, cut:
★ 2 squares, 8½" × 8½" (24 total)
★ 6 squares, 5" × 5" (72 total)

From the white solid, cut:
★ 9 strips, 8½" × 42"; crosscut into 36 squares, 8½" × 8½"
★ 18 strips, 5" × 42"; crosscut into 144 squares, 5" × 5"

From the blue print, cut:
★ 10 strips, 2½" × 42"

Note: You'll have some leftover 5" squares; we've cut extra to ensure you'll have enough matching squares per block.

Hunter Star by Melissa Corry

FINISHED QUILT: 96½" × 96½"
FINISHED BLOCK: 16" × 16"

Making the Blocks

To make sure you have enough matching and contrasting pieces for each block, arrange your print squares before sewing. Group each print 8½" square with two matching 5" squares. Make 36 groups. Then chose one 5" square from a second print and one from a third print for each group. You'll also need a white 8½" square and four white 5" squares. Keep prints together as planned by making one block at a time.

Press all seam allowances as indicated by the arrows.

1. Draw a diagonal line on the wrong side of four white 5" squares. Place a marked square right sides together with a print 5" square. Sew ¼" from both sides of the line. Cut along the line to yield two half-square-triangle units. Using the seamline as a guide, trim the units to measure 4½" square, including seam allowances. Repeat to make four units that match the large print square and two other pairs of half-square triangle units.

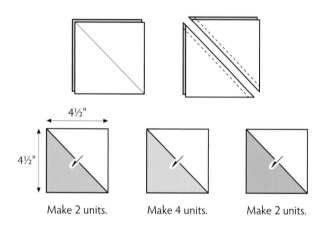

Make 2 units.   Make 4 units.   Make 2 units.

2. Lay out the large print and white squares and the half-square-triangle units from step 1 as shown. Make sure the units that match the large square are positioned by the large square. Join the half-square triangles in each group of four to make two units that measure 8½" square, including seam allowances.

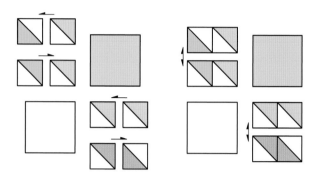

3. Join the pieced units and squares in each row, and then join the rows. The block should measure 16½" square, including seam allowances. Repeat to make a total of 36 blocks.

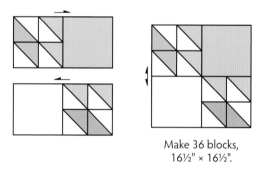

Make 36 blocks,
16½" × 16½".

PLAN AHEAD

These blocks are relatively easy to sew, but the beauty of the design depends on good color placement. If you have a design wall, arrange your units on it before assembling the blocks. If you don't have a design wall, the floor or the top of a bed can come in handy.

Assembling the Quilt Top

1. Lay out the blocks in six rows of six, rotating them as shown below to create the star design. Rearrange the blocks as desired until you are pleased with the mix of prints and colors.

2. Join the blocks in each row, and then join the rows. The finished quilt top should measure 96½" square.

Finishing the Quilt

Go to ShopMartingale.com/HowtoQuilt for more details on quilting and finishing.

1. Layer the backing, batting, and quilt top; baste the layers together. Hand or machine quilt. The quilt shown is machine quilted with parallel lines in the stars and an allover loop design in the background.

2. Use the blue 2½"-wide strips to make the binding and then attach it to the quilt.

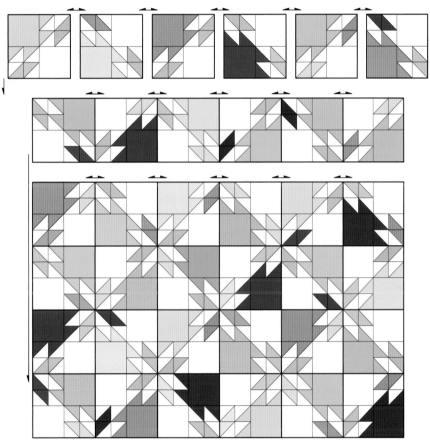

Quilt assembly

Woven Star

Play with a cool palette of blues to make a sleek, modern design featuring nine small Star blocks surrounded by a calm gray background.

Materials

Yardage is based on 42"-wide fabric. Fat quarters measure 18" × 21".

5½ yards of gray solid for blocks and negative space
1¼ yards of light blue solid for blocks and binding
⅓ yard or 1 fat quarter of dark blue solid for blocks
¼ yard or 1 fat quarter of medium blue solid for blocks
6⅔ yards of fabric for backing
80" × 98" piece of batting

Cutting

All measurements include ¼" seam allowances.

From the *lengthwise* grain of the gray solid, cut:
★ 1 rectangle, 40" × 72½"
★ 1 rectangle, 15" × 72½"

From the remainder of the gray solid, cut:
★ 1 rectangle, 10½" × 36½"
★ 1 rectangle, 26½" × 36½"
★ 36 squares, 3½" × 3½"
★ 9 squares, 7¼" × 7¼"

From the light blue solid, cut:
★ 4 strips, 3⅞" × 42"; crosscut into 36 squares, 3⅞" × 3⅞"
★ 9 strips, 2½" × 42"

From the dark blue solid, cut:
★ 2 strips, 4¾" × 42"; crosscut into 9 squares, 4¾" × 4¾"

From the medium blue solid, cut:
★ 2 strips, 3⅞" × 42"; crosscut into 18 squares, 3⅞" × 3⅞". Cut each square in half diagonally to yield 36 triangles.